The Baggywrinkle Cookbook

Sarita Armstrong

© Sarita Armstrong 2014 – Copyright Owner

No part of this book may be reproduced in any form or by any means electronic or mechanical, including recording or by any information storage and retrieval system without permission in writing from the author. Sole exception is in the case of brief quotations embodied in critical articles or reviews.

Paperback ISBN: 978-1-910088-10-4

Ebook ISBN: 978-1-910088-11-1

sarita@saritaarmstrong.com

www.saritaarmstrong.com

info@sifipublishing.co.uk

SifiPUBLISHING

WWW.SIFIPUBLISHING.CO.UK

www.sifipublishing.co.uk

In the old days sailors tied the unwanted frayed ends of rope with a half-hitch around the shrouds of their sailboats and packed them tightly together. The fluffed-out ends formed a soft cushion to prevent the sails from chafing on the shrouds. This was known as a Baggywrinkle.

A Baggywrinkle also became an endearing term for a sailor 'who knew a thing or two'. He knew by instinct when a storm was brewing or when to set fair sail. He knew when to take in a reef on the mainsail and when to shake it out. He did not need a wind-gauge to tell him how hard the wind was blowing, nor which direction it was coming from. He could feel it on the back of his neck or his ears. And he did not need a GPS to tell him when to change course.

Captain Bill Baggywrinkle of this book ('Baggy' to his friends) is a composite character. Circumstances forced him to learn to cook for himself and he applied the same instinct of knowing when something was ready, knowing when it was at its best – or its worst – to his cooking.

All the characters are fictional. The stories are based on experience but we don't have to spoil a good story for the sake of the truth, do we?

This book is dedicated to Martin with whom I shared the storms and the tranquil seas.

My thanks again to Simon Fraser for all his help and encouragement.

When I was a teenager it was with some shock I realised I was most probably going to have to spend my adult life cooking every day for a husband and family.
At the same time it occurred to me that the more you know about something the more interesting it becomes. This instigated my interest in culinary skills and has benefitted me throughout life.

TABLE OF CONTENTS

> ✓   simple to prepare and cook.
> ☐   keeps well and/or re-heats.
> *   good enough for entertaining.

AN INTRODUCTION TO BAGGY   1

CHAPTER 1   THE SINGLE-HANDED COOK   5

The Baggywrinkle Stand-By ✓   7
Baggy's Bosun ✓   8
Baggy's Bootlace ✓   10
Baggy's Bulgur Stir-Fry ✓   10

CHAPTER 2.   THE VERSATILE OMELETTE   12

French Omelette with Cheese and Tomato ✓   14
Baggy's Bacon & Garlic Omelette ✓   15
Greek Potato & Spinach Omelette ✓   16
Spanish Omelette ✓   17
Baggy's Bouffant Omelette 'Fine Herbes' ✓   19

CHAPTER 3: THE CHILLED OUT CHEF — 21

Champion Chicken ✓ ☐ * — 23
Baggy's Beery Beef Casserole ✓ ☐ * — 24
Herbed Dumplings ✓ * — 26
Posh Pork ✓ ☐ * — 26
Chicken Pot Roast ✓ * — 27

CHAPTER 4: THE ROAST DINNER — 29

Basic Recipe for Roast Meat with Vegetables & Gravy ✓ * — 31
Roast Pork ✓ * — 33
Roast Lamb ✓ * — 34
Roast Beef ✓ * — 34
Roast Chicken ✓ * — 35
Fresh Herb Stuffing for Chicken ✓ * — 36
Roast Shoulder of Lamb ✓ * — 37
Vegetarian Roast ✓ — 38

CHAPTER 5: ALL THE LEFTOVERS — 40

Baggy's Bonne Femme ✓ ☐ * — 42
Rice ✓ ☐ — 43
Savoury Stuffed Pancakes ☐ * — 45
A Simple Duxelles Sauce ✓ * — 47
Fried Borek Rolls ✓ — 47
Chicken or Meat Pie ☐ * — 48

CHAPTER 6:   SOMETHING OUT OF NOTHING — 49

Grandma Baggywrinkle's Cornish Pasties ☐ — 51
Potato & Onion Flan ☐ — 53
Quiche Lorraine ☐ * — 55
Stuffed Cabbage Leaves ☐ — 56
Bread & Butter Savoury Pudding ✓ — 58

CHAPTER 7:   TOO MANY MACKERELL — 60

Mackerel Fried with Ouzo ✓ ☐ — 62
Greek Sardines (fried in garlic) ✓ — 63
Anchovies ✓ — 64
Baked Salmon with Parsley or Dill Sauce ☐ * — 65
Fishmonger's Pie ☐ * — 67
Mild Fish Curry with Coconut ✓ ☐ * — 69

CHAPTER 8:   UP THE CREEK — 71

Baggy's Bolognaise Sauce ✓ ☐ — 73
Baggy's Beefburgers ✓ ☐ — 74
Chilli con Carne ✓ ☐ — 75
Rabbit à la Moutarde ☐ * — 76
Bacon & Chicken Livers on Toast ✓* — 78
Chicken Liver Pâté ✓ ☐ * — 78

CHAPTER 9:   NIGHTWATCH — 80

Nightwatch Cake ☐ * — 82
Rock Buns ✓ — 83
Scones ✓ — 84

Flap Jacks ✓ ☐ 85

4 x 4 Sponge Cake * 86

CHAPTER 10: THE SQUIRREL INSTINCT **88**

Garlic Mayonnaise (Aioli) ☐ * 90

Pickled Eggs ☐ 91

Orange Marmalade with Coriander ☐ 92

Blackberry & Elderberry Jelly ☐ * 93

Pesto ✓ ☐ 95

Pickled Capers ✓ ☐ * 96

Ginger Beer ☐ * 96

Hot Sweet Chutney ✓ ☐ 98

CHAPTER 11: ALBERTINA **99**

Albertina's Spaghetti ✓ ☐ 101

Spaghetti alla Carbonara ✓ 102

Moussagna ☐ * 103

Liver in Orange Sauce ✓ * 106

CHAPTER 12 : THE RAT RACE **107**

Fish Pâté ✓ ☐ * 109

Prawns in Garlic & Cream Sauce ✓* 110

Gougière * 111

Pastry Puffs * 112

CHAPTER 13: TURKISH MARKET — 114

Market Day Pie ☐	116
Braised Chard with Pistachio Nuts ✓*	118
Buttered Carrots Braised with Onion ✓ *	119
Spinach in Yoghurt ✓ ☐	120
Tomatoes Stuffed with Bulgur ✓☐	121

CHAPTER 14: BEAUTIFUL SOUP — 123

Cream of Mushroom Soup ☐ *	125
Mixed Vegetable Soup ☐	126
Cream of Lettuce Soup ☐ *	128
Leek & Potato Soup ☐	129
Fresh Tomato Soup ☐ *	129
Jerusalem Artichoke & Mussel Soup *	130

CHAPTER 15: ENTERTAINMENT — 132

Honeyed Fruit Salad ✓ *	134
Crème Delight ✓ *	134
Mrs. B's Apple Crumble ✓ * ☐	135
Strawberry Sponge Flan *	136
West Country Treacle Tart ☐ *	138

INDEX TO TIPS & TECHNIQUES — 141

ABOUT SARITA ARMSTRONG — 147

AN INTRODUCTION TO BAGGY

Old Captain Baggywrinkle's son was known as Bill Baggy in his home village, or affectionately as Baggy to his friends. It was a name that always brought a smile with it, for he grew up long and lean with not a trace of bagginess about him. He was the kind of man who would walk into the pub in his gumboots bringing with him the aura of night seas and gales. He had the dark blue long-distance eyes of the seafarer and the calm self-confidence of a countryman. His undeniable charm was enhanced by a complete unawareness of his attractiveness to the opposite sex.

But he wanted a better life than a declining West Country fishing port could provide, so he left the rocky coast to make his fortune in the city. This was some years ago, long before his mid-life crisis when he decided that he must return to the element that had always sustained him: the sea.

Throughout his working life his spare time had been spent with boats despite the moans of his wife and children when he drove them down – yet again – to the coast for a week-end of sailing. But now he was determined to do it seriously. For an excellent price he sold his assets, which by this time amounted to a fine house and a flourishing business, and bought a sea-going sailing yacht of sturdy proportions. He renamed it *The Sea Crow* much to his wife's annoyance for it had been called *The Maid of Beaulieu*. The rest of the money he invested wisely.

"We can sail around the world for ever," he told his wife, "living off the interest without even touching the capital." (This was in the good old days when bank interest rates were interesting).

Betsy Baggywrinkle was bravely enthusiastic. She tried to forget about those wet and bumpy Channel crossings, thrashing to windward for the Monday morning office deadline. She dreamed instead of lazy days sunbathing on the deck in the tropical sunshine, listening to the distant sound of Caribbean drums, a fresh lime juice tinkling with ice in a glass at her side. But moving out of her home and packing away all her treasures wrenched at her heart. Though Baggy himself was anxious that the boat should be comfortable and have room for lots of homely items, a great many things had to be left behind. It was hard too to leave her grown-up children who still seemed so young and defenceless. They promised to come and stay for their holidays but she knew it would never be the same again.

After a busy summer preparing the yacht, they set off in the autumn. They headed across the Bay of Biscay towards the Canaries, ready to cross 'the puddle' and gain an extra summer in the Caribbean. But the Bay of Biscay lived up to its reputation for bad weather and lumpy seas so they put in to Lisbon to dry out and recuperate. It was here that Betsy insisted on a change of plan: they should head for the Mediterranean (an area that seemed relatively close and connected to home) in order to find their sea legs. Her husband reluctantly agreed.

So winter found them in Palma, where Betsy soon made friends with like-minded wives who were none-too-keen on the seafaring life their husbands had chosen. It was not long before a wealthy middle-aged ex-patriot whose wife had recently absconded with the local barman, rescued Betsy from what she was beginning to feel might be a fate worse than death. He showed her his villa with the bougainvillea around the door. He walked with her along his terraced garden with the orange trees. He sat with her by the secluded swimming pool and together they watched the sunset view from the balcony. The ice tinkled in the glass at her side, and she thought she caught the distant sound of drums … somewhere … Within a few weeks she had packed her bags and quit *The Sea Crow*.

Baggy was desolate, but determined. On reflection, he found he quite liked the thought of sailing off on his own with no one to nag him, no one to disagree with his route or his choice of anchoring spot. He ignored the pile of dirty laundry growing in the corner of his luxurious aft-cabin; but after some days as he ate his dinner – cold baked beans spooned from the can as he leant over the sink to catch the drips – he decided it was time to take himself in hand.

He emptied the rubbish, scrubbed the galley and took the washing to the launderette. Then he sat down with the few cookery books his wife had inadvertently left behind. But it was all a mystery.

'Make a roux …' one recipe began. 'Mix to a smooth batter …' said another. '… dropping consistency,' pronounced a third.

"It's beyond me!" Baggy grumbled. "There must be an easier way." So he put the books aside and decided to do it in his own way - and he made a few notes as he went along.

Many years later one of Baggy's grown-up daughters came to stay on the boat. In her tidying up she found a sheaf of cookery notes that had fallen down behind the chart-table. When she saw the unexpected contents of the crumpled, grease be-splattered pages, she rummaged again and found yet more notes relating to food-preparation: how to do this, what to remember about that, what changes to make, and so on.

She started to put them into some order then added a few comments of her own. And here it is -

The Baggywrinkle Cookbook

CHAPTER 1   THE SINGLE-HANDED COOK

Baggy's eyes wandered to the heap of empty cans casually cast aside in the galley and whilst he had to reprimand himself for his laziness, he could not help but consider the absence of washing up they represented. He could choose to eat whatever took his fancy and there had been no: "your turn for the dishes, dear," to spoil his meals. But he was nearly through the stock of cans they had so carefully stored away for their Atlantic crossing and he was only too aware that this way of life could not continue.

What he needed was a meal with a minimum of washing-up. He reckoned no-one required more than one cooked meal each day so he would concentrate on one meal cooked all in one pan – and eaten from the pan too, if necessary. Since he was in Spain he thought he would try to cook a paella, not realising how complicated it might be; so first thing in the morning off he went to the local market to purchase some stores. He had never enjoyed shopping and whilst Betsy rummaged for the best buy he would stand gazing over the heads of other shoppers looking as though his mind was somewhere else entirely, which it probably was, each hand weighed down with shopping bags and his back aching.

This time it all seemed different, for he was on a mission. After gazing at the colourful heaps of cabbages, carrots and beetroot, and ignoring the gap-toothed old woman who tried to sell him a kilo of walnuts and the young bread-vendor who wanted him to break his teeth on a crusty loaf, he wandered on to the fish market where – luckily for him – he found a stall selling ready-mixed ingredients for paella 'sold by the scoop.' Before he knew it, the lovely young girl behind the counter had inveigled him into buying a couple of scoopfuls plus some delicious-looking prawns.

Back on the boat he could not wait until dinnertime so decided to experiment for lunch. All the ingredients – peas, seafood, rice, bits of squid and mussels - had more or less de-frosted on the journey home. He piled it all into a frying pan with some oil and twirled it around, then realised he would have to add some water. On top he placed the special prawns. It simmered slowly on the lowest heat whilst Baggy watched attentively the development of his first meal. During his waiting he wanted to do something, so added something colourful from a small jar – it could have been paprika or saffron – he wasn't sure. He poured himself a glass of wine while he waited, adding a slurp from his glass to the mixture as it burbled slowly away.

"I think I could enjoy this," he said to himself, giving the paella a gentle stir and pouring another glass.

But he was in trouble – it was all sticking on the bottom and becoming stodgy; moreover the wine bottle was nearly empty! By the time it all seemed ready it must have been three o'clock in the afternoon, but Baggy did not care for he had been absorbed in what he had been doing. He felt the occasion deserved the laying of a knife and fork and a place mat on which he placed the somewhat sooty frying pan and proceeded to eat his way through the contents straight from the pan. It was not very good but it was the first hot meal he had eaten in ages. He felt like a king at a banquet.

Tomorrow, he decided, he would cook something similar but in his own style and then each day he could vary the ingredients – endlessly. Instead of rice he could use noodles, or pasta, or even potato. Without knowing it, he had invented his own stir-fry: The Baggywrinkle Stand-by.

RECIPES

The Baggywrinkle Stand-By ✓

Utensils
1 saucepan
1 frying pan
1 or 2 gas rings

Ingredients
1 large potato
2 rashers of bacon
½ leek
½ red pepper, diced
1 clove garlic, crushed
A knob of butter
A pinch of salt & black pepper
A dash of sherry
Slices of cheese

Method

1. Peel the potato and cut it into roughly mouthful sizes. Cook in boiling water for 5 minutes.

2. Meanwhile, cut the bacon into pieces; melt the butter in the frying pan then add the bacon pieces.

3. Wash the leek, cut it into 1" pieces. Add them to the pan.

4. Add the crushed garlic and chopped red pepper; salt and pepper. Stir

TIPS & TECHNIQUES

The idea of this book *is to encourage you to cook for yourself and for others in a relaxed, enjoyable way.*

Recipes *marked with* ✓ *indicate they are simple to prepare and cook.*

Recipes *marked with* ☐ *indicate they keep well and may be re-heated.*

Recipes *marked with* * *indicate they are good enough for entertaining.*

The recipes are for two people *unless otherwise stated. Most meals will bear re-heating, so if cooking for yourself only, you may as well make a double portion and eat it again another day. It reduces the amount of cooking you do in a week. Some meals actually improve with keeping.*

Ingredients *are listed in the order in which they are used in the recipe.*

Although exact measurements are given in the recipes, your cooking will be much simpler if you can learn to manage by measuring as little as possible. It saves time, it saves

occasionally and if it seems to be sticking, add a little water from the potato pan.

4. Drain the potato; add it to the other vegetables and continue cooking until the leeks are soft.

5. Add a splash of sherry and turn the heat up briefly.

6. Remove the pan from the stove and stir in the cheese slices so they just begin to melt as you serve it up.

Baggy's Bosun✓

Utensils
1 saucepan
1 frying pan
1 or 2 gas rings

Ingredients
A large handful of pasta
3 - 4 oz (100 g) thinly-sliced fresh meat or a few thin slices of cold left-over meat
½ onion
½ red or green pepper
3 medium-sized mushrooms
½ a stock cube melted in ½ cup of water taken from the boiling pasta.
A dash of sherry
Salt & pepper

washing up.

Baggy did all his cooking without a set of scales. He soon learnt to judge when he needed a slurp of this or a dollop of that, a handful of rice or a sprinkle of spice.

If you find you do not have a certain item, don't worry – perhaps you can use something else? For instance, in the recipe opposite, if you do not have two slices of bacon you could try using salami or chorizo sausage. If you don't have a leek, an onion will do just as well.

Do you need a little water for your stock cube? Perhaps you already have some boiling the potatoes or pasta?

When cooking pasta or potatoes always cook more than you need so that you have enough for another meal. They will keep well in the fridge and you will have some ready for the next day so you only need the one pan for the meals in this section.

We are told these days that reheating rice is bad for you because rice contains a bacterium that can multiply if left at room temperature. But so long as you have put it in the fridge as soon as it is cold and make sure it is well re-heated, you should come to no harm. This applies to any

Butter/olive oil
1 level tbsp plain flour

<u>Method</u>

1. Bring a pan of salted water to the boil and throw in the pasta. Cook for 10 - 15 minutes.

2. Chop the vegetables into large pieces.

3. Melt a knob of butter or some olive oil in the frying pan. Add the vegetables and cook until the onion is soft but not collapsed.

4. If using fresh meat add it at this point and cook until no pink is showing.

5. Sprinkle the vegetables with the plain flour to absorb the fat. Add the stock cube mixed with the ½ cup of water and stir.

6. If using cooked meat, add it now. Splash in sherry and raise the heat briefly. Cook until the meat is well heated through.

7. Drain the pasta and gently mix it with the ingredients in the frying pan.

food you are going to re-heat.

Some Basics *for your store-cupboard: salt, pepper, cooking oil, plain flour, rice, pasta, stock cubes, mixed herbs, potatoes, onions, carrots, garlic.*

Chopping onions *without tears: first peel the onion (to be fool proof under a running tap). Cut the onion in half from top to bottom and place it flat side down on your chopping surface.*

Cut slices length-wise, holding the onion in shape with your left hand. Turn the onion 90° without lifting it and cut again.

The form of the onion has done half the work for you and the tear-jerking juices remain within the flesh until it is ready for the pan.

To make onion rings: *cut the whole onion the opposite way after peeling.*

Mushrooms *enhance a dish much more if cut from crown to root, both in looks and in maintaining their distinct flavour.*

Alternatively, if you want the mushroom flavour to blend in a dish, (as in a casserole), then chop them finely so that the flavours blend.

Baggy's Bootlace ✓

For a vegetarian version of either of the above, omit the meat and alcohol. Stir in two soft-boiled eggs, cutting them as you go so that the yolk runs out. Add fresh parsley, chervil or 'Fine Herbes'. (See T & T page 19). Sprinkle with grated cheese.

Baggy's Bulgur Stir-Fry ✓

Utensils
1 frying pan
1 gas ring

Ingredients
½ green or red pepper
½ onion
½ courgette
½ fennel bulb
Butter size of an egg
1 clove garlic
3 - 4 oz (100g) beef, veal or pork in thin slices and/or a handful of nuts
½ cup of Bulgur
1 cup of stock made from boiling water and stock cube
A pinch of chilli powder
Salt and pepper
Fresh parsley or coriander

The same principle applies to onions which taste quite different if merely cut in quarters rather than finely chopped before cooking.

__A clove of garlic__ is one segment from the bulb.

__A garlic crusher__ will crush a clove of garlic even if it is not peeled.

Baggy had no such new-fangled implements, so he crushed his garlic cloves with the flat of a broad-bladed knife – squashed like a fat white bug – after which he found them easier to cut up finely with the same knife. Easier to deal with when dead, he thought, rather than skittering around as they did before the flat-bladed treatment.

He also discovered that a little salt added to the clove when he squashed it made it softer and encouraged the juices to exude.

__Leeks__ are best prepared by first removing any leaves or ends that you do not want to eat, then cutting lengthways from the green end until one third of the way through the white part.

Wash them carefully under a running tap with the leaves pointing downwards so that any grit is washed out rather than into the leaves.

Method

1. Chop vegetables in bite-size pieces.

2. Melt the butter in the pan, add the vegetables and squeezed or finely chopped garlic and cook until the onion begins to brown. Add the meat slices, turning briefly.

3. Add the bulgur and stock. Stir and cover firmly. Remove from the heat until the liquid is absorbed.

4. Raise heat briefly, add the chopped parsley or coriander, and fluff up the bulgur with a fork.

Serve with garlic yoghurt
(see page 120)

For more vegetable preparation information see page 116.

Bulgur *is a very nutritional cereal made from the starchy centre of wheat grain, so contains a lot of protein. It is largely ignored in western countries, but is a staple food of the Middle-East and North Africa, where it is usually found in the form of Couscous.*

It has been known since ancient days and is easy to cook, providing a cheap form of protein ideal for vegetarians. It may be served hot, or cold as a salad with a garlic dressing.

CHAPTER 2.   THE VERSATILE OMELETTE

The winter gales grew less and the sun developed some generous warmth as the days grew longer. Baggy spent his days in harbour getting his boat ship-shape again, varnishing here and painting there, greasing sea-cocks, checking ropes and sails, changing oil filters and such-like down in the engine room.

When at last the weather seemed settled though there was still a cool breeze in the air, he set off for the other end of the Mediterranean. He had considered following his original plan of crossing the Atlantic, but the season had passed and now he was alone. Anyway, he liked the ambiance of the Mediterranean countries. He was not in a hurry, but neither was he keen on hanging about; something of which he felt he had already done too much.

It was a wrench to think that his lovely wife and mother of his children was finally left behind, but he turned his blue eyes to the horizon, set the course and raised the sails. It was a beautiful day and the waves splashed and sparkled on the bow as *The Sea Crow* cut through the blue water. There was plenty to keep him occupied and the feeling of being on the move again filled him with eager anticipation. He intended to stop each night whenever possible for he knew that tiredness could cause accidents, and being alone there would be no one to help him out. Anyway, he wanted to see the places on the way. Besides this, he had no intention of eating his dinner with the wheel in one hand and a spoon in the other.

The first evening he stopped in a deserted bay and simply dropped the anchor. It was a different world from the bustle of harbour life. *The Sea Crow* also had a different feel about her as she rocked gently to her chain. Baggy was peacefully tired so he did not bother with anything grand for dinner. He poured himself an 'anchor-dropping drink' and feeling totally at peace with the world as he sipped it, he watched the stars pop out of the darkening sky one by one. At last he went below and cooked himself a Spanish Omelette, which he considered to be a meal in itself. When it was ready he took it to the cockpit and sat in his favourite seat, his plate and glass on the cockpit table.

The calmness of being at anchor surrounded by nothing more than hills covered in rough vegetation filled him with a gentle peace after the day's activity. The absence of companions made him feel more in tune with his boat and the environment and it crossed his mind that he might turn into one of those crazy lone sailors. He wondered if he should procure a cat as a companion: a ship's cat – a sea-cat - but then he thought of the paddy paws on his work-tops, the little nose sniffing at his fish pie, and decided against it.

By this time he had experimented with a variety of omelettes and considered himself to be quite proficient in their production. Many swear words had been uttered during the learning process and many burnt and scrambled eggs had been eaten or thrown away (depending on the time of evening). But now that he had it sorted, he took great pride in producing what he liked to call a French omelette.

RECIPES

French Omelette with Cheese and Tomato ✓

(For one person)

Utensils
Bowl and fork for whisking the eggs
Small frying pan or omelette pan
A fish slice
1 gas ring

Ingredients
1 oz. (28 g) grated cheese (a lump the size of a small egg)
½ tomato chopped
2 eggs
Salt & pepper
Oil or butter

Method

1. Beat the eggs in a bowl with a fork and add the salt, pepper, cheese and tomato.

2. Heat the oil in a pan until it is just beginning to smoke. Turn the heat right down and pour the egg mixture into the pan.

3. With the fish slice push the cooked egg from the edge of the pan to the middle whilst tipping the pan so that uncooked egg re-covers the bare part.

TIPS & TECHNIQUES

A French Omelette is a fancy name for an English Omelette, such as we all know from childhood. The French purloined the name because they considered they were the only people capable of making it to perfection, a claim that may be somewhat out of date.

A Fish Slice is an essential kitchen tool that does not necessarily have anything to do with fish. Everyone knows this implement which is more often used for turning eggs or beefburgers in a frying pan. They come with a long unmanageable handle, but Baggy's favourite was one he had sawn the end off so it could be used without banging his elbow on the bulkhead every time he fried an egg.

The success of an omelette depends on a) getting the pan hot enough before you pour in the egg mixture, b) immediately turning down the heat, and c) pushing the edges to the centre and tipping the pan so that uncooked egg fills the empty part of the pan.

When Baggy became more adept at his omelettes he found he could dispense with the fish slice and simply roll his omelette up with the

Adjust the heat if it seems slow, remembering that the whole cooking process should only take a couple of minutes.

4. Before all the egg is quite cooked, flip one half over the other and leave it to rest on the lowest heat for a minute or so.

Baggy's Bacon & Garlic Omelette ✓
(For one person)

Utensils
Bowl and fork for whisking the eggs
Small frying pan or omelette pan
1 gas ring

Ingredients
1 - 2 rashers of bacon
1 small clove garlic
2 eggs
Ground black pepper
A little oil or butter

Method

1. Cut the bacon rashers into 1" pieces and chop the garlic finely.

2. Beat the eggs with a fork, season with pepper.

3. Melt a little butter or oil in the pan and fry the bacon and garlic together.

fork with which he had whisked the eggs.

Eggs are not all the same, as Baggy knew only too well. Free-range eggs cost extra money but are more solid in texture and decidedly better for you. The quality of the egg depends on the quality of the food that the chicken has been eating. A 'scratcher' that has been roaming around the yard picking up all sorts of meaty protein and fresh herbs will produce a lovely firm egg with a dark yellow or orange yolk, a firm translucent white, and a solid shell that does not shatter into pieces when you try to crack it. Such a free-roaming hen will be less highly medicated with antibiotics so the eggs will be less adulterated.

A free-range egg is also much easier to manage. In a frying pan it will hold together with the yolk standing high. A poor-quality battery egg will spread across the pan with the white running away, especially if it is old. The yolk also will be pale and flat.

One disadvantage of a fresh egg is that when hard-boiled it will be difficult to peel, with the shell holding onto the white. A stale egg peels easily and has a large air space at one end.

Since battery eggs got a bad name for the conditions in which the

4. Turn down the heat and immediately pour in the egg. With a fish slice mix it quickly with the bacon then move it from the edge to the centre allowing the raw mixture to flow over the uncovered pan area.

5. When almost all the egg is cooked, flip one half over the other, turn off the heat and allow the omelette to rest for one minute.

<u>Alternative combinations</u>:
   Mushrooms and garlic
   Bacon and mushrooms (and garlic)
   Bacon and tomato
   Cheese and onion

Cheese and tomato may be added to the egg. Other ingredients should be cooked first.

Greek Potato & Spinach Omelette ✓
(For one person)

<u>Utensils</u>
Bowl and fork for whisking the eggs
1 shallow frying pan or omelette pan
1 saucepan
1 gas ring

<u>Ingredients</u>
A handful of fresh spinach
Olive oil
Cooked potato cut in small chunks

hens were kept, we now have many more supposedly free range hens' eggs on sale, but this is often not the real thing. It may only mean the hens are allowed to range a little more freely out of their coops now and then and the food they eat is just the same as before.

On the other hand, just because you buy your egg from a farmer does not mean the hens are necessarily free range. Baggy received some very suspect produce from farms in his efforts to find good free range eggs.

If food sticks in the frying pan because– like Baggy's old one – it is not of the non-slick variety and refuses to release anything you put into it without a struggle, here's what to do to improve the pan:

Sprinkle salt into the empty pan and heat it to a high temperature, shaking the salt about in it as you do so.

Or: cover the base of the pan with olive oil and again heat it until it smokes and the oil penetrates the metal. Leave it to cool then wipe it clean with kitchen paper.

Or: throw it out and invest in a new non-stick pan.

Whenever feasible, simply

2 eggs
Salt & pepper
A sprinkle of Parmesan cheese

Method

1. Wash and cook the spinach for a few minutes in a saucepan, with only the water that clings to the leaves. It will shrink alarmingly. Squeeze out any excess water and chop the leaves.

2. Fry the potato in the oil until just starting to brown.

3. Beat the eggs and add the spinach to it with the salt and pepper.

4. Add the egg mixture to the potato and mix a little so that the egg is mostly cooked.

5. Divide the omelette in half and flip each half over in the pan. (You can do it all in one piece but it may break up).

6. Serve sprinkled with the parmesan cheese.

Spanish Omelette ✓
(For one person)

This is the most substantial of the omelettes and can be made with any left-over vegetables, fish or shellfish.

wash with water and wipe your frying pan clean with kitchen roll rather than using washing-up liquid.

It is preferable to have two pans: one flat pan for frying and for omelettes, the other deep and with a lid, for stir-fries and the many dishes that begin with oil and end up with liquid added. It is the liquid that ruins a frying pan.

Butter or Oil *can be used for an omelette. Butter is preferable for a delicately flavoured dish, otherwise olive oil or a combination of the two, works very well. Butter burns at a lower temperature than oils. Olive oil has the highest non-burning heat resistance, so a little olive oil added to the butter will help to stop the butter from burning.*

Tomato skins *may be removed if you prefer. This is simply done by dipping them in hot water for a minute and then removing the skin with a sharp, pointed knife. You may have some potatoes or pasta on the boil already, in which case you can dip the tomatoes in the pan rather than boiling water especially for the purpose. They will be too hot to handle, so oink them out with the pointed knife and let them cool a bit before peeling.*

A Greek Omelette, *like a Spanish omelette, is a solid affair,*

But traditionally it contains peas and cold potato, small lumps of cheese and chopped tomato.

Utensils
Bowl and fork for whisking the eggs
Frying pan or omelette pan
Lid or tin foil
1 gas ring
(Grill)

Ingredients
2 eggs
Chopped cold potato, chopped tomato, cheese chopped in small lumps, cold peas
Half a teaspoon mixed herbs
Salt & pepper
A small clove of garlic crushed
A little olive oil

Method

1. Beat the eggs and add salt, pepper, herbs and garlic.

2. Heat the olive oil in the pan, add the egg mixture, and sprinkle the other ingredients on top.

3. As before, pull the edges to the centre, then leave on a very low heat without turning it over. Cover with a lid or tin foil to help the top cook before the bottom is too well done.

4. Finish it off under a grill if necessary.

quite unlike the delicate type that we know in England. Try not to overcook it – it should be firm but not leathery on each side, yet soft in the middle.

Boiled potato *is often best re-heated in another recipe, and keeps well covered over in the fridge. So if you are boiling them for one recipe always cook a few extra for another day.*

Whisks: *there are many types of whisk, both electric and hand-operated.*

For beating egg for a normal omelette you need nothing more than a fork and a small bowl.

For whisking egg whites there is nothing better than a balloon whisk, as traditionally used by good French chefs. The bubbles obtained are larger than an electric whisk can make, so the end result is altogether lighter and fluffier. You need a good large bowl too.

An electric whisk will do the job without much physical effort on your part.

To separate egg white *from the yolk is not a job for the faint-hearted, but the omelette is very forgiving so it is a good time to practice. Professional chefs seem to do it with the egg white sliding through*

Baggy's Bouffant Omelette 'Fine Herbes' ✓

(For one person)

Utensils
A bowl big enough to whisk the egg whites
A small bowl for the egg yolks
A balloon whisk or electric whisk
1 shallow frying pan or omelette pan
1 gas ring

Ingredients
2 eggs
Salt and freshly ground black pepper
Chives or the green part of a spring onion, chopped
Fine Herbes or Tarragon
A knob of butter
A sprinkling of Parmesan or other grated cheese (optional).

Method

1. Separate the whites of the eggs from the yolks (see T & T)

2. Beat the egg whites until they are light and fluffy but not hard then fold in the yolks, herbs, salt and pepper.

3. Heat the butter in the pan until just starting to brown, then immediately pour in the egg mixture.

4. Proceed as before, moving the

their fingers, but it seems a very messy way. Instead, the egg shell itself can be put to use.

a) Have two bowls ready - a large one for the egg whites and a small one for the yolks.

b) Crack the egg on the side of the large bowl and allow the white to slither out while you hold the yolk back with the shell edges. Now tip your egg yolk into the small bowl.

When Baggy's daughter read her father's notes she felt sad at all the trouble he had gone to. Modern technology had a much simpler answer to the problem of separating egg yolks from their white – she had seen it on U-tube! An empty plastic water bottle was all that was required.

Break the whole egg into the large bowl for the white; squeeze the bottle to expel a little air from it then suck the egg yolk gently into the bottle and puff it out again into the small bowl. Poor Dad!

If you do get bits of yolk into the whites it will make it difficult if not impossible to make them fluffy. But a bit of white in the yolk will not matter much.

'Fine Herbes' *can easily be purchased in a small jar from a good supermarket, but of course are much*

mixture from the edge to the centre and encouraging the uncooked mixture to re-cover the pan.

better if fresh from the garden, herb pot or hedgerow.

They are a mixture of any of the following herbs: parsley, sweet marjoram, chives, chervil, mint, coriander, dill.

These are all gentle or 'fine' flavoured herbs ideal for the delicate flavour of the soufflé omelette.

CHAPTER 3: THE CHILLED OUT CHEF

Whenever Bill Baggy arrived at a port, he did not let the other 'yachties' along the quay know about his culinary hobby. While they heated a can of beef stew for their meal, Baggy was busy in his galley experimenting with this and that. They were unaware that his shopping bag contained not only bread and salami but also fresh mushrooms, chard, globe artichokes and a variety of unusual items he had discovered in the local market. The rattling in his carrier bag was not just caused by beer bottles but also by little jars of herbs and spices.

He was wise in his reticence, for as a single man he had plenty of invitations to dinner on other yachts where the wife or girlfriend would take great pleasure in giving him what she assumed would be his only decent meal of the week. Although this was by no means the case, he was still delighted to be fed by someone else whilst being absorbed into the gentle atmosphere of dinner on board in harbour.

Those living on yachts spend much time alone so are always glad to socialise when they reach port. There would be a sense of uniqueness as one stepped from the quay crowded with holiday-makers onto a yacht moored stern-to, a bottle of wine or a bunch of flowers in hand. Inside, the light of an oil-lamp might give a gentle glow to the woodwork, just glimpsed through a porthole by passers-by, as the boat swayed gently to the wash of harbour traffic or to a gentle swell from rough seas outside that would not reach beyond the harbour wall.

During those evenings he was very interested in the business, or busy-ness, of his hostess in the galley, and it made him realise how relaxed he had become about his own cooking. Having discarded the cookery books before he had even begun, he had not been inhibited by the niceties of accuracy. Since he did not possess any scales he had not bothered with weighing and measuring. Timing was something he did by looking and tasting. Never had he hurried over his cooking, always having had more than enough time in the long evenings to prepare his meal. He always poured himself a glass of wine or an aperitif while he cooked, which rather turned the chore into an event in his mind.

If something looked as though it would be ready before the rest of the meal, he simply turned it off and found that some dishes were actually improved by having a rest. The herbs and spices seemed to blend better with a little more time allowed for them. Even a bolognaise sauce could be made at any time and left to mull until he decided it was time to eat. In fact, pasta, rice, potatoes and even carrots came to little harm if they were brought to the boil and simply turned off or removed from the stove to make room for another pan while they continued cooking slowly in their own heat, at the same time reducing the energy consumption. The main meal could be cooked in advance and simply re-heated. The slow cooker too came into its own.

So by the time Baggy found it necessary to return the hospitality he had received, he was able to conjure up a perfectly acceptable meal and present it without too much huffing and puffing beforehand.

RECIPES

Champion Chicken ✓ □ *

(For 4 people)

Utensils

A large deep frying pan (wok) or wide shallow saucepan with lid
A large flat plate
1 gas ring

Ingredients

6 chicken portions or 1 whole chicken cut into chunks and seasoned with salt, pepper and thyme
1 tsp grated lemon rind (optional)
Olive oil
1 onion quartered
1 clove garlic chopped or crushed
1 red or green pepper in large chunks
1 courgette cut in pieces
Chicken stock cube melted in a cup of boiling water
A handful of shell pasta or macaroni
Tarragon or mixed herbs
Cornflour mixed to a cream with white wine or dry sherry.

Method

1. Put a good splash of olive oil into the pan and brown the pieces of chicken in it. Remove them to a plate and sprinkle

TIPS & TECHNIQUES

The idea behind this chapter is that some dishes taste a lot better when the ingredients have had time to rest and blend.

These recipes *use basically the same method and are an adaptation of the peasant hot pot that can be found in various guises all over the world where all the ingredients are cooked together in one pot over a fire, from the billycan stew of the Australian outback to the Laplander's pot-reindeer. However, there is nothing wrong with giving this simple meal an up-market twist, as many nationalities have done: the British casserole, the cassoulet of France, the goulash of Hungary.*

If using the recipes for entertaining serve them with separate fresh vegetables.

In all these recipes the meat may be seasoned up to 24 hours in advance and left to mature before cooking.

When cutting meat *for a casserole always prepare it carefully by removing gristly bits and fat.*

You may prefer to buy a chunk

with the lemon rind.

2. In the same pan lightly fry the onion, pepper and garlic, adding more oil if necessary.

3. Return the chicken to the pan with the vegetables; add the tarragon or herbs and the stock. Bring to the boil, cover with a lid then reduce the heat and simmer for a minimum of ½ hour.

4. Half an hour before serving, add the courgette pieces and the handful of pasta.

5. Raise the heat; add the cornflour and wine/sherry and let it come to the boil so that the gravy thickens. Season to taste, then reduce the heat again and serve whenever you are ready.

Baggy's Beery Beef Casserole ✓□ *

(For 4 people)

Utensils
1 large bowl for the beef
A large deep saucepan
1 gas ring

Ingredients
1½ lbs (700 g) beef cut into chunks
½ small can or bottle of beer, preferably dark

of meat and cut it up yourself - that way you can remove sinews and any bits you don't want to eat from the whole piece and simply cube the good bits. This is easier than trying to re-do little chunks that have been previously prepared badly by a butcher.

One larger piece of meat will keep better too, rather than one cut into small pieces.

Mixed Herbs *are the most commonly used herbs and are the stronger version of 'Fine Herbes' mentioned above. Used in all Mediterranean cooking, they are usually a mixture of thyme, oregano, rosemary and bay leaf. A jar of mixed herbs, often called 'Herbes de Provence' is essential in a kitchen, though if you can find them fresh they are so much better.*

The use of dried herbs is assumed in these recipes unless fresh ones are specified.

The inclusion of the pasta helps to thicken the gravy.

Dry Sherry *is a very useful addition to many dishes instead of wine and gives it a certain 'up market' flavour.*

Dried Beans *such as flageolet beans, kidney beans, butter beans,*

1 clove garlic, crushed
Mixed herbs, salt & pepper
1 onion in quarters
2 carrots cut in pieces
1 green pepper in large pieces
4 oz (110 g) mushrooms
1 beef stock cube or 1 level tsp Bovril
1 small tin flageolet beans

Method

1. Put the beef, garlic, herbs and seasoning into a bowl and pour the beer over it all. Mix well and leave to stand for two hours or preferably overnight.

2. Put a little oil in your saucepan and heat. Squeeze as much liquid out of the meat as you can and brown the meat in the oil.

3. Add the chopped onion, carrot and green pepper and fry lightly.

4. Add the rest of the liquid and the stock or Bovril. Bring briefly to the boil then reduce the heat to a simmer, covered with the saucepan lid.

5. Half an hour before serving add the tinned flageolet beans.

chick peas, lentils and so forth are a good staple to have in the cupboard, but in my experience that is where they are most likely to remain. It is such a chore to soak them and then cook them before adding to a recipe, that it is one of the few foods that are best used from the a tin.

Tinned foods *are looked down on by 'a good cook' – but there were some that Baggy liked to have in his store cupboard.*

These were tinned tomatoes to use in a sauce; tinned sweet corn, which has its uses to bulk out a dish; as do Chinese bean sprouts. Tinned red kidney beans, large white butter beans and flageolet beans are all useful if you have no time or inclination to prepare the dried ones. They are useful for adding to other dishes and are a good source of protein.

If using tinned beans always remember to add them to the dish at the end of the cooking, otherwise they are likely to become stodgy.

These dishes may make a lot of liquid if left to cook with the lid on. Use the lid by removing or replacing to decrease or increase the liquidity of the contents of the pan.

These days we are accustomed

Herbed Dumplings ✓*

Mix 4 oz (112 g) of self-raising flour with 2 oz (56 g) of fat or Atora suet and some herbs, salt and pepper in a small bowl. Add a little water so that you can form the mixture into small balls. Drop the balls into a casserole, replace the lid and let them cook in the gravy. Beware: they will double in size.

Posh Pork ✓ □ *

(For 4 people)

Utensils
A large deep frying pan (a wok is ideal)
1 bowl for the meat
1 gas ring

Ingredients
1½ lbs (700 g) good pork meat cut in bite sized pieces
Salt, pepper and marjoram (or mixed herbs)
Olive oil
1 onion, chopped
1 clove garlic, crushed
1 green pepper, chopped
4 oz (110 g) mushrooms, sliced
1 cup stock (stock cube + boiling water)
A dash of dry sherry
Cornflour

to having our food rather glutinous, and it is good to have the gravy thick enough to coat the other ingredients. Cornflour mixed with a little cold liquid then added to the pan and brought to the boil will achieve the same result without the need for the artificial additions that we find in all packaged foods.

Any of these recipes may be transferred to a casserole dish after browning in the pan then cooked in a conventional oven. For some reason this improves the flavour and texture and has the advantage that you can serve it to your guests straight from the casserole dish.

***The slow cooker** is a useful piece of equipment on a boat or caravan if you have an inverter that converts the battery power to normal electricity. This allows you to use the power created by your engine when moving along to cook your dinner, which should be ready to eat on arrival at your destination. What could be better?*

***A Pressure Cooker** had been left on board when Baggy purchased his boat, but he never managed to get good tasting food out of it, and whilst it may have its uses, he felt it had no place in a book of recipes.*

If you find you have a lot of

Method

1. Mix the meat in a bowl with the flour seasoning and herbs. Leave it to stand for at least an hour.

2. Fry the onion, garlic and pepper lightly in some olive oil. Push to one side and add the meat cubes, browning them on all sides.

3. Add the stock and the mushrooms; bring to the boil then reduce the heat to simmer. Cover with a lid or not, depending on how much liquid is forming. Cook for ¾ hour.

4. At the end of the cooking time add the sherry, mixed in a cup with some cornflour if the gravy is too thin. Bring it briefly to the boil again to thicken it.

Chicken Pot Roast ✓ *

Utensils
Wok with lid or similar pan large enough to hold a small chicken
1 gas ring

Ingredients
1 small whole chicken with drumsticks and ends of wings removed
A bunch of fresh herbs (rosemary, thyme, tarragon, oregano)
Oil and butter mixed

liquid in your casserole, you can add dumplings and double the size of your meal!

For a hearty pie, you can use the same recipes without the pasta or beans and cover it with pastry. Bake in the oven until the pastry is brown and crispy. (See page 53 for pastry).

If the casserole dish looks rather full, place it on a flat baking tray or put tin foil on the bottom of the oven. Then if it does overflow it is easier to throw away the tin foil or wash an extra pan rather than having to clean the oven or suffer the smoke from burning grease.

Removing the drumsticks: *cut the legs through the 'knee' joint, leaving the 'thigh' attached to the body.*

The reason for doing this is that the remainder of the chicken is compact and cooks evenly.

The drumsticks can be used in another dish, or added to the pot roast separately.

Quail *can be cooked in this way very well because they are so small. They fit well in the pan and stay moist.*

With the lid on, a certain amount of liquid is made in

Bacon pieces (optional)
1 onion, halved crosswise
2 carrots
2 potatoes

Method

1. Put the onion halves and herbs inside the chicken. Brown the chicken on all sides in the wok with the oil and bacon. Add the vegetables cut into large chunks.

2. Season with salt and pepper. Put on the lid and cook slowly for 20 minutes. Turn the chicken over and cook for a further 20 minutes. If necessary continue cooking with a slightly higher heat until clear juices come out of the thigh when poked with a sharp knife.

condensation and keeps the meat moist.

Heating the plates *for a meal usually gets forgotten until the last minute when you are in a rush with everything else, so you don't bother. However, it is well worth doing, since it keeps the food warm whilst you are serving up and certainly should be done if you have guests, when everything takes a little longer. Last minute heating of plates can be done quite simply by placing them over a saucepan in which you are boiling vegetables.*

CHAPTER 4:   THE ROAST DINNER

These top-of-the-stove meals were all very well, but there came a time when Bill Baggy had a yearning for a proper Sunday lunch or more specifically for a roast dinner. It had been a long time since he had sat down with his family around a Sunday roast then lazed away the afternoon in idle chatter. It was the whole atmosphere of the well-laid table, a carefully prepared meal, and the gathering together of the family that he missed. The conversation that accompanied the food was more important than the accompaniments to the roast joint.

Here in the Mediterranean countries he noticed the families gathered together much more than in England. They joined in an old-fashioned way over long meals at large tables, or large meals at long tables that held three generations of family members who talked together in an animated gabble: young boys listening attentively to grandmothers, young mothers talking animatedly to grandfathers, toddlers being helped to their food by spinster aunts, teenage boys laughing and joking but never over-stepping the formality of the occasion.

He saw them in smart restaurants, he glimpsed them in country gardens under overhanging vines, he passed by them on wide verandas: he noticed them everywhere and always felt a sudden emptiness somewhere between his heart and his gut. He yearned for that unselfconscious acceptance of the family bond that spanned the generations.

He had been talking to his friend Giorgio, asking him in a roundabout way about Mediterranean cuisine, and Giorgio had told him, "For us it is not the food that is so important. No! It is the conversation that ensues from joining friends; the wine that loosens the tongue; and lastly the food – though of course it is the food that makes the occasion."

Oh! How he missed all that! He could join acquaintances in the taverna, but it was not the same at all. So, although he was alone on his boat, he still wanted to keep his English traditions and cook a big joint of meat. It would be wasteful for one person, he thought, but when he was a bit more practised he could have a dinner party. Though who would he invite? Then he considered all the dishes he could prepare with the left-overs - that is, if he could resist the temptation of pinching bits out of the fridge in the middle of the night. Oh, why did stolen meat always taste so much better than when it was served up on a plate?

So, in a welter of nostalgia he put some oil in a roasting pan and heated it in the oven, then added his joint of meat - a small round of pork he had chosen at the butcher - sprinkled with salt, pepper and herbs. He surrounded it with peeled and halved potatoes, making sure all was covered with the oil, and put a piece of tin foil on top to stop the splatters in the oven. When it was sizzling away he turned the oven down, added a large peeled carrot, and spooned the fat over everything again.

After an hour, with mouth watering from the smell, Baggy poked a knife into the meat and only clear juices appeared so he knew it was cooked. By this time the potatoes were reasonably brown (though not as crispy as he would have wished) and the carrot just soft. He turned the oven off and quickly sliced some cabbage finely, throwing it into a little boiling water. He boiled it furiously for a few minutes.

Baggy removed the sizzling goodies from the roasting tray to a plate and covered them with the tinfoil again to keep warm. As he carefully poured the fat out of the tray into a bowl he realised that a lot of meat juices were lying beneath, so he saved them and sprinkled a spoonful of flour into them, added the water from the cabbage and mixed it into smooth gravy.

It seemed a lot of bother, although he was pleased to notice that he had only used two pans, yet he sat down to a feast of roast meat, roast potatoes, carrots, greens and gravy. If only he had someone to share it with! He also realised that he had the where-with-all for another couple of meals, not to mention all that cold meat just waiting for his midnight temptation!

RECIPES

Basic Recipe for Roast Meat with Vegetables & Gravy ✓ *

Utensils
Roasting tin
Heatproof bowl for the fat
I small saucepan
Oven full on, then gas mk. 5
1 gas ring

Ingredients
Approx. 2 lb (1 kilo) joint of meat, (or a whole, prepared chicken)
3 potatoes, peeled and halved
1 onion, halved crosswise
1 carrot
½ cup oil
1 tbsp flour

Method

1. Pre-heat oven to gas mark 6.

2. Heat oil in the roasting tin in the oven then add the prepared joint (see individual recipes) and turn it over so it is sealed on all sides. Add the potatoes.

3. After ½ hour reduce the oven temperature to mk. 5. Add the carrot and onion. Baste everything with the oil.

TIPS & TECHNIQUES

Crispy Roast Potatoes - it is always a problem to get them done by the time the meat is ready. There are several reasons for this:

a) When our English cooking traditions evolved large joints of meat were roasted for several hours. This gave the potatoes time to cook and become crispy and brown. But nowadays our small joints of meat are cooked before the potatoes have a chance to brown.

b) The meat came from animals that had been raised naturally on pasture, so the meat contained less water than today's joints. Watery juices that exude from a joint of meat produced from factory farming - and especially if it has been frozen - prevent the potatoes from crisping up.

There are ways of helping the potatoes to brown:

a) If the potatoes still look a bit anaemic when the meat is ready, remove them to a completely dry roasting tin, or a small baking tray then raise the oven heat as high as possible. They should brown while you make the gravy. You will be amazed at how much fat comes out of them too.

4. Cook for 15 - 20 mins per lb weight of meat, spooning fat over the meat at intervals.

5. Test for readiness by poking the meat with a sharp knife or skewer. Chicken and pork should exude clear juices. (Poke chicken in the thigh). Lamb and beef can have slightly pink juices if you like the meat rare.

6. Remove the meat and vegetables to a large plate and keep warm, wrapped in tin foil.

For the Gravy:

1. Tip the corner of the roasting tray over a heatproof bowl and gently pour off the fat, or spoon it out, leaving the residue of meat juices in the tin.

2. Sprinkle the flour into the juices over a low heat on top of the stove and stir gently. Pour a teacupful of hot water or stock, or water from the greens into it and stir, pressing out any lumps with the spoon. Simmer for 1 - 2 minutes. This makes a thick gravy.

3. If you prefer thin tasty gravy, you can make a demi-glace sauce with the juices. Instead of the flour, add a glass of wine (red for red meat; white for white meat) then turn the heat up high and stir, scraping all the brown bits off the pan and allowing much of the

b) You can simply roast the potatoes in a separate tray, allowing them extra time from the start, but in this way you do not get the proper taste of a roast potato done in the meat pan. It will help if you can use lard or fat from a previous joint.

c) You can boil the potatoes until half-done; drain them and shake them in the pan before adding them to the roasting tin.

d) Some people have been known to shake the potatoes in a plastic bag containing flour before putting them in the roasting tin. The flour absorbs any extra moisture on the potato, helping to crisp it.

e) Microwave the potatoes for two minutes before placing them in the roasting tin. This also dries them out, helping them to brown.

A Microwave oven *was not an option for Baggy, but many yachts and caravans now have one and they are extremely useful, especially for reheating dishes.*

Place the potatoes *in the pan with the rounded side down. If you put the flat cut side down first they will be likely to stick to the pan. You can turn them over later.*

The Oven on a yacht *or in a*

liquid to evaporate until you have a nice rich sauce.

For a tasty joint of meat it is best to season the meat before cooking. This can be done a day or an hour in advance.

Roast Pork ✓*

Seasoning
Mustard (preferably Dijon)
Garlic (crushed)
Sage or mixed herbs
Salt & pepper

Method

Spread Dijon mustard, or any prepared mustard, over the outside of the joint. Rub in the crushed garlic, salt, pepper and a little sage or mixed herbs.

Vegetables
Roast it with carrots, potatoes and halves of fennel root.

Accompaniment
Mustard Sauce: make a white sauce, (see page 104); add a teaspoon of mustard and a dash of wine vinegar.

caravan may be small. It may only have a knob marking full, medium, low and off, in which case the temperatures given in these recipes may mean very little.

When you place something large in a small oven the temperature will reduce considerably, so always pre-heat the oven. In practice a small oven may need to be on almost full for most of the time.

When roasting a joint of meat in the oven, pre-heat it then keep it on full until you hear the meat sizzling in the fat. Then you can reduce the heat, but turn it back up again if the sizzling dies away - otherwise you may wait forever for your dinner!

Be aware that you may be placing your roasting tin directly over a high flame at the back of the oven, so anything at the back may have a tendency to burn on the bottom. It may be the best place to put the potatoes.

The Best Gravy *is made only from the juices of the meat. If you have to add a stock cube because there are not enough juices from the meat, remember you may only need to use ½ a cube so you do not over-power the meat flavour. You can save the rest of the cube for another time.*

Roast Lamb ✓*

Seasoning
Garlic
Rosemary
Cumin
Salt & black pepper

Method

Spike the meat at intervals and insert a sliver of garlic and a small sprig of rosemary. If there are natural breaks in the meat (between lean and fat) use these breaks. Sprinkle a small amount of cumin powder over the joint, as well as salt and pepper.

Vegetables
Roast the joint with potatoes, carrots and parsnips.

Accompaniment
Mint Sauce or Jelly; or Redcurrant Jelly.

Roast Beef ✓ *

Seasoning
Olive oil
Garlic
Thyme and/or oregano; or mixed herbs.
Salt & black pepper

Seasoning: I have not given quantities for the seasonings but be warned not to over-do it to start with. It should enhance the flavour of the meat rather than over-powering it.

Rosemary *is a lovely herb that grows everywhere as a fragrant bush and can often be found in gardens and growing wild. Pick it whenever you can and hang it up to dry, or put some sprigs in a small glass of water where it will keep fresh for a long time. It goes well with all strong meats.*

Bay. *The same applies to this herb which grows as a small tree or bush, often spreading over the wall from a derelict garden. Keep the leaves whole - they make a useful addition to many dishes.*

Cumin *- a very distinctive spice - is typical of middle-eastern dishes and should be used with caution until you grow accustomed to it. It is used especially with lamb and goat. It comes in whole seeds or ground. In these recipes use the ground form.*

Pork Crackling *- that old-fashioned English delicacy – so often it fails for no fault of the cooking. It is to do with the type of meat, especially the cut.*

We are so anxious these days

Method

Mix the seasoning ingredients together and rub it into the meat.

Vegetables
Roast it with potatoes, whole onion, and parsnips or chunks of sweet potato.

Accompaniment
Horseradish Sauce

Roast Chicken ✓ *

Seasoning
Whole onion, peeled and halved
A sprig of fresh thyme
A sliver of lemon rind
Melted butter
Crushed garlic
Paprika

Method

1. Place the halved onion, thyme and lemon rind in the body cavity.

2. Combine the melted butter, garlic and paprika and rub the mixture into the skin.

Vegetables
Potatoes, carrots, celery

to eat healthily that most joints of meat contain very little fat.

In Cyprus they produce the most delicious pork you will ever have tasted, for they feed the pigs on the residue from the wine production. Happy pigs!

To make crackling *first you must buy a joint not only with skin on the edge, but with a layer of solid-looking fat between the skin and meat. This is how meat always used to be and you can still find it on certain cuts (e.g. Ribs).*

Score the fat with a sharp knife first one way then across the other way, to make a diamond pattern. For ribs score it in the same direction as the rib bone.

Rub a thin coating of oil over it with your hand or a pastry brush then sprinkle it with salt. (If doing this, do not add the mustard as advised in the recipe).

Oil and Cooking Fats:
traditionally a roast would be cooked in lard or dripping (fat used on a previous roast). Now we are more health conscious most people would prefer to use oil. However fashions change and many people are beginning to wonder about the highly manufactured oils produced for cooking.

Accompaniment
Bread Sauce:

Put some soft white breadcrumbs into a small saucepan and add ¼ of a finely chopped onion; salt, 4 whole black peppercorns & a pinch of nutmeg. Cover with milk, add a knob of butter or margarine and cook as slowly as possible until the milk and bread are combined, stirring occasionally to check it is not burning on the bottom.

Fresh Herb Stuffing for Chicken ✓ *
This makes twice the meal out of a roast chicken.

Ingredients
A small bowlful of white bread-crumbs
A knob of butter or margarine
¼ onion, finely chopped
1 teaspoon of mixed herbs
Plenty of fresh parsley, chervil, or a small amount of fresh coriander leaf
1 clove garlic, crushed
A small piece of lemon zest finely cut or grated.
1 beaten egg

Method

1. Rub the fat into the breadcrumbs.

2. Mix in all the other dry ingredients

Baggy preferred to use natural olive oil since it was comparatively cheap in Mediterranean countries. The locals he met used it in huge quantities yet did not seem to suffer from cholesterol problems. It is now becoming cheaper everywhere with the growing demand.

Nevertheless, Baggy could not resist saving the fat from his roast and using it again when making dishes with the leftover meat for he knew it contained a great deal of flavour and goodness.

After all, as a child he used to come home from school to a chunk of toast and dripping – the fat and meaty jelly piled on a piece of toast – and he had not suffered from it!

Giblets: *those pieces of chicken that often come stuffed inside in a plastic bag. On a mass-produced bird one should be aware that any hormones or antibiotic residues collect in the liver, as they do in the neck where the birds are injected.*

Chicken liver *is nevertheless a real delicacy and hard to resist. Chopped and quickly fried, it makes an excellent addition to the Fresh Herb Stuffing.*

Stuffing for Chicken. *These days one is advised not to put stuffing*

then add the egg and combine it all into a loose ball.

4. Place under the flap of neck skin of the chicken, or in the body cavity. (See T & T).

5. Roast the chicken as above.

Roast Shoulder of Lamb✓ *

Utensils
Roasting tin or casserole dish
Tin foil
Gas oven pre-heated to mk.5

Ingredients
Shoulder of lamb and vegetables, all prepared as for Roast Lamb above.

Method

1. Place a piece of tin-foil large enough to wrap around the joint lengthways in the roasting tin then place a similar piece cross-ways.

2. Put a little oil on the tin foil, then place the vegetables on it and the joint of lamb on the vegetables.

3. Seal the tin foil so that no juices can escape.

4. Place in the pre-heated oven and

in the body cavity of a chicken, as it can lead to salmonella poisoning. However, this is only because of the way a frozen chicken may have been kept before you bought it and is a modern problem due to mass marketing.

If you are buying fresh chicken from a good source there should be no reason not to put stuffing in the body cavity where it will flavour and moisten the whole bird. Rinse out the cavity and dry it with kitchen roll.

If you prefer you can put the stuffing under the flap of neck-skin, but it has a way of oozing out and does not permeate and moisten the flesh in the same way.

Stuffing things is a wonderful way of making the meal special whilst at the same time making so much more of it.

***Soft white breadcrumbs** can be rubbed from the loaf with your hands, or made with an electric mixer or liquidizer.*

***Dried Breadcrumbs** can be purchased in packets, or you can make your own golden breadcrumbs out of stale bread.*

***Golden breadcrumbs** that may keep for ever can be made by*

reduce the heat (gas mk 3). Roast (in fact you are almost steaming) for approx. 1 ½ hours, or until the meat is well cooked and falling from the bone.

5. Roll back the tin foil and raise the oven heat as high as possible, to brown the joint and potatoes. You will be surprised how quickly it all browns up, though you may like to remove the potatoes to a separate dish (see T & T p. 31)

6. Remove the meat and vegetables to a separate plate and make the gravy as above.

Vegetarian Roast ✓

Utensils
Roasting tin or casserole dish
Gas oven mk. 5

Ingredients
A mixture of any of the following:

Potatoes or sweet potatoes (small or quartered), carrots, parsnips, swede, turnip, cauliflower sprigs, quartered fennel root, red or green peppers (de-seeded and chopped in quarters), onions (peeled and quartered).
Whole sprigs of fresh rosemary and/or thyme
A sprinkling of sweet paprika

drying out the bread in a low oven. (Pop it in when you have turned off the oven having finished cooking something else). Then crush the dried bread with a rolling pin or a wooden spoon. Store it in an airtight jar or tin, so it is always to hand when you need it.

Stuffing can be varied according to whatever you have available, or whatever takes your fancy.

Cooked rice could replace half of the breadcrumbs. Finely chopped red or green pepper and/or chili could be added.

At a dinner where one or two people may not like to eat much meat, make plenty of hefty stuffing with the addition of chopped nuts.

You can, place it in a separate greased dish or baking tray and serve it with roast pork.

Alternatively, serve it with the vegetarian roast opposite, to make a full vegetarian roast dinner.

Steam-Roasting *as for the shoulder of lamb can be used for any joint of meat that you expect to be a bit on the tough side. The meat cooks slowly in its own juices and the goodness remains in the pan.*

Olive oil
A little salt, plenty of black pepper

Method

1. Prepare the vegetables and heat the oil in a roasting tin or casserole dish.

2. Mix the vegetables and herbs in the roasting tin and roast for ½ hour, adding more oil if necessary and turning the vegetables as required.

It has the same affect as the completely enclosed ovens traditionally used in primitive cultures.

Vegetables that we did not like when served up on their own can be so much better when roasted whole in this recipe.

Typical examples are parsnips and swede, which take on a sticky sweetness when cooked in this way.

CHAPTER 5: ALL THE LEFTOVERS

It had been a downwind sail, so Baggy had not really noticed how much the wind had increased in strength. He had been enjoying steering for a change after the autopilot had decided the rolling waves on the stern were too much for it to cope with. The sun was getting low but soon he would round the point and motor into the large bay to anchor for the night in the shelter of the top-most corner. He was surprised to see two coasters taking shelter at anchor in the entrance to the bay and reckoned the wind must have grown stronger than he had realised, or else there had been a bad weather forecast.

Confident as ever, he rounded the point and switched on the motor while he rolled away the genoa. Two minutes later, with a cough and a splutter the engine died.

"Must be air - or muck in the fuel," he reckoned. "All this rolling about could have stirred it up from the bottom of the tank."

If he were to sail all the way up the bay it would take until after dark, tacking to and fro, so he raised his trusty staysail and let *The Sea Crow* set her own course gently across the bay while he went below to check filters and bleed the engine.

Leaning over the hot motor Baggy cursed and sweated. He never could find the right sized spanner; there was never enough light to see by; the smell of diesel was making him queasy. He was worried about the boat's position and every so often he would jump up from what he was doing and stick his head out of the hatch in order to check it. Would they get past the coasters with all the leeway *The Sea Crow* was making with her small sail? He eyed it up and reckoned they would just skim by, but kept an ear open for anything untoward as he worked away below.

At last he was ready to try the engine again. He pushed the starter button for what seemed like an age. Would the battery die before the engine burst into life?

"Come on, come **on** ..." he coaxed under his breath. "Yes!" With a judder, a shake and then a roar the engine fired. He dashed below again to make final adjustments to the bleed screws then gently coaxed the boat towards the anchorage.

He could just make out the shoreline in the gathering dark and thankfully dropped the anchor in five metres of clear water over a level sandy bottom. Grey clouds were gathering over the hilltops and he could smell bad weather in the air. He fretted over the engine problem. It should not have happened and it worried him to be at anchor with a dodgy engine.

"Ah, well," he sighed. "It's dinner time. Perhaps I shall feel better after something to eat."

He went to the fridge but there was only leftover pieces from his roast dinner - and there was not much of that. He cut a chunk of meat and slapped it between two hunks of bread liberally spread with butter. Then he sat munching morosely in the cockpit with his hands imparting an aroma of diesel to the sandwich. At last he started to unwind and to take his mind off more important matters began to ponder on the other things he could have done with his leftovers.

The meat did not have to be put between slices of bread and butter. It could be wrapped in - well, pastry for instance, or a pancake. What about a pasty - just like old Grandma Baggywrinkle used to make? Or simply added to a lovely creamy sauce. He would think it over - but not tonight.

RECIPES

Baggy's Bonne Femme ✓ ☐ *

<u>Utensils</u>
Medium saucepan with lid
1 gas ring

<u>Ingredients</u>
¼ cold cooked chicken or scraps from the carcass.
Butter the size of a small egg
1 rasher of streaky bacon, chopped in pieces (optional)
½ onion or leek chopped
¼ red pepper, diced
½ clove garlic, crushed
2 pink-gilled mushrooms, chopped
1 tbsp flour
1 cup milk
½ chicken stock cube melted in ½ cup boiling water or left-over chicken gravy + a dash of sherry
A little parsley, sweet marjoram, or tarragon

<u>Method</u>

1. Tear the chicken meat from the bone and cut it into bite-size pieces.

2. Gently heat the butter in a saucepan; add the bacon pieces if using them, and add the prepared onion or leek; cook until the onion is translucent. Add the mushrooms and garlic and continue

TIPS & TECHNIQUES

Baggy's Bonne Femme is based on the traditional French recipe with a few changes.

Pink-gilled mushrooms *or young mushrooms should be used in any creamy dish rather than ones where the gills have turned dark, for dark-gilled mushrooms will discolour the sauce. Alternatively, you can use any of the pale Oriental mushrooms now on the market, such as Shitake.*

Leftover Gravy *- even if you only have a tablespoonful, it will impart a much more genuine and healthy flavour to the dish than a stock cube. The jelly that collects around a cold joint can also be used.*

Stock Cubes *for adding to the water in which you cook your rice: these have their uses but can be a bit overpowering. They are fairly heavily endowed with monosodium glutamate, otherwise known as 'flavour enhancer' so those who suffer with this should beware.*

Tarragon *– a very French herb –makes a welcome change to the herbs in the Bonne Femme recipe.*

Prepared garlic *in tubes or jars is available these days, though it seems a bit silly to have it in stock when the real thing is so readily*

cooking for 2 minutes or so.

3. Sprinkle the flour over the vegetables and stir well. Add the milk, stirring all the time.

4. Now add the gravy or stock and the chicken pieces. Cook gently, stirring occasionally for 5 - 10 minutes. Check seasoning and add salt & pepper if necessary.

5. Add the herbs at the last minute. If you have left-over stuffing, however little, add this too.

Serve on a bed of rice with a sprinkling of diced tomato or green peas to give it colour.

Rice ✓ ☐

<u>The simplest way</u>

1. In a large pan, boil plenty of water and throw in the rice. Add a little salt.

2. Bring the water back to the boil and stir the rice to make sure none is sticking to the bottom of the pan.

3. Simmer for 15 minutes. Drain and serve.

available. But sometimes when you only want a little flavouring and it seems such a bother to get out a chopping board or a garlic crusher, it is good to be able to slip a bit out of the tube when no-one is looking.

__Ginger__ in a tube works in the same way.

__Harissa__ is ready-prepared chili in a tube. It lasts for ever. Very handy.

__Sherry__ in cooking is wonderful and gives an up-market flavour to dishes that might otherwise be a little bland. Dry sherry gives the same flavour as dry white wine, but more so, and will not thin down a sauce.

__Rice:__ the first method is fool proof so long as your pan is large enough and well filled with water.

Plain boiled rice can be the best accompaniment to offset a tasty dish. Heavily seasoned rice may fight with the flavours of a dish, especially delicate ones such as the Bonne Femme.

Where the flavour of the rice is important Baggy would use the second method. He found the result to be tastier than the other method and no more difficult once he got the hang of it. The amount of water needed may

Another method

1. Put a kettle of water on to boil. Take a saucepan with a lid and heat a little oil in it.

2. Measure your rice, (an average mug will be ample for two people) and add it to the oil. Heat and stir until the rice begins to turn white.

3. Add double the quantity of boiling water as you did rice. It will bubble and splutter as you add it but that's OK. Add a little salt and put the lid on firmly, turning the heat down to a minimum.

4. Leave for 15 minutes but check every now and then that it is not sticking to the bottom of the pan and if necessary remove it from the heat altogether. Rice has to cook very gently this way, but it will be done in 15 - 20 minutes.

To cook rice in a microwave

1. Take half a mug of rice and soak it in cold water for 30 minutes.

2. Drain and rinse the rice, then add 1 mug of cold water and a little salt and oil.

3. Microwave for 9 mins. Leave to stand in the microwave oven for 5 minutes.

vary slightly depending on the rice used.

The addition of a little chopped onion to the oil together with the rice helps to keep it moist and flavoursome.

As with pasta, if you find you have ended up with a sticky mass: drain the rice, boil up some fresh water and rinse the rice in it. This is also a good way of re-heating leftover rice. (That's when you have leftover leftovers).

If you buy half-cooked rice, follow the instructions provided on the packet.

If convenience is of prime importance, the boil-in-the bag rice is excellent.

Use long grain rice for savoury dishes and try to use good quality rice even if it costs more. There are so many different varieties on the market - try different ones just for a change.

Rice can be cooked very successfully in a microwave but in this case the quantities and timing must be exact.

Saffron *makes all the difference to the look of a risotto or paella because it gives the rice that lovely golden colour. It comes from*

Savoury Stuffed Pancakes ☐ *

You can make this with the leftover leftovers, yet it is still good enough for entertaining.

Utensils
Balloon whisk (not essential)
A large plate
A wide flat casserole or oven-proof dish
A small frying pan or omelette pan
1 or 2 gas rings
Oven, preheated to gas mk. 5

Ingredients
A quantity of Chicken Bonne Femme mixed with some cooked rice.
A small tin of condensed mushroom or asparagus soup; or one cup-a-soup made fairly thick.
A little cream or crème fraise
A sprinkling of Parmesan cheese

For the batter: (which should be made at least ½ hour in advance).

4 oz (110g) plain flour
1 egg
1 pt (½ l) milk
A pinch of salt

Method

1. Make the batter by putting the flour into a small mixing bowl. Break the egg

the stigmas of a purple crocus and was grown widely in England in the Middle Ages as well as by the Romans. Saffron Walden takes it name from this plant. It is supposed to cheer you up and I dare say the Romans needed it in cloudy Albion!

It can be found in powder form or in little packets of the stigmas themselves. Always infuse it well in the liquid you are using to get the full benefit.

***Stuffed Pancakes** can be made with the leftovers from the Chicken Bonne Femme recipe, including any rice and/or vegetables.*

Pancakes may be stuffed with anything. For a change, the recipe given here is excellent if the chicken is substituted for fish and/or seafood, with asparagus soup.

Instead of the rice you can add sweet corn, or make it oriental with bean sprouts. A vegetarian version could be made with all these.

Instead of the soup, for an upmarket version, you can make a classic Sauce Duxelles. A simple version is given here.

On a rainy afternoon why not settle in and make some tea-time pancakes rolled up with honey and lemon juice?

into it; add the salt and a little of the milk. Mix it round (preferably with the balloon whisk, but a wooden spoon will do) so that it forms a thick paste. Add more milk gradually until it is the consistency of thick cream Leave it to stand for ½ hour preferably in a refrigerator.

2. Heat the chicken & rice mixture and have a plate ready for the pancakes. Also have the casserole dish to hand with a ¼ of the soup spread over the bottom.

3. Put a very little oil in the pan and heat it until it starts to smoke. Stir the pancake mixture and pour enough of it into the pan to cover the bottom thinly.

4. Shake the pan about, turn the heat down then lift the edge of the pancake as soon as you can with a fish slice. Be brave and turn it over. Cook the other side then lift it onto the plate.

5. Continue making the pancakes until you have as many as you want.

6. Spread two or more spoonfuls of the chicken mixture just to one side of the centre line of a pancake, roll it up and place it in the casserole dish. Continue with the rest of the pancakes.

7. Mix the cream or crème fraise with the rest of the soup and pour it over the

Pancake Batter is a very useful item to be able to make. No bread? No cake? Make a pancake! Don't know what to do with something? Put it in a pancake.

Although quantities are given for the recipe opposite, you do not need to measure the quantities for batter. Put a good handful of flour in a bowl, mix in the egg and a little of the milk then just keep adding the milk and stirring it in until it is the consistency of thin cream. Make plenty rather than too little, because you can always keep it and use it later.

When making batter always make more than you think you will need for the recipe. There is nothing worse than not having quite enough for your needs, and if you have extra left over it can happily sit in the fridge ready for those tasty teatime treats.

Batter should stand for at least half an hour, and can wait a day or more if necessary. This enables the gluten in the flour to combine with the liquid and stick it all together.

The first pancake you make invariably goes wrong. You just have to accept that the pan seems to need the first one to get into gear. The last one is always the best, and that's

top of the pancakes in the casserole dish. Sprinkle a little Parmesan cheese on top and bake in the pre-heated oven for ½ hour or until the sauce bubbles and the cheese is brown on top.

A Simple Duxelles Sauce ✓*

Fry in plenty of butter some finely chopped shallot or onion; add finely chopped mushrooms and continue to cook until soft. Take up the butter with a little flour sprinkled into it, add a little stock and simmer for a few minutes. Add cream, season to taste.

Fried Borek Rolls ✓

Utensils
Frying pan
1 gas ring

Ingredients (makes 8)
A quantity of pancake filling (as above)
A standard round of borek pastry, cut into 8 equal slices, as you would cut a round cake.
Oil for frying

Method

1. Place a tablespoonful of the filling onto the wide end of each section; roll

usually the one the cook eats!

Do not at this stage attempt to get the pancakes beautifully thin, and forget about tossing them. Just be happy that they are all in one piece.

When you are proficient at making pancakes you will find you can stuff and roll at the same time as cooking the next pancake.

***Duxelles Sauce** is the posh version to be used rather than the instant cup-a-soup mix. But it is one extra thing to do when there is quite a lot of work in the stuffed pancake recipe anyway.*

***Filo or Borek Pastry** - filo in Greece, borek in Turkey - but basically the same paper-thin pastry that can be bought ready prepared and comes in large round circles.*

It has many uses, from the traditional sweet baklava pastries, to the finger-size savoury rolls used as a snack or starter, or the large pies with layers of vegetables and meat between the layers of pastry.

Although the pastry is delicate, it is surprisingly easy to handle. For the fried borek recipe opposite, or for any of the 'finger' boreks, cut the round as you would a cake.

Place a little filling at the wide

once to cover the filling; turn in the ends like a parcel, then continue to roll it up to the pointed end. (See T & T).

2. Heat the oil in the frying pan and place the rolls in the pan with the pointed end underneath to seal them.

3. Fry the rolls gently on a low heat, turning as required so that they are brown all over and the filling is heated through.

Chicken or Meat Pie □ *

Make the basic Bonne Femme Recipe above and put it in a pie dish. Cover with rolled out packet pastry or your own home-made short crust pastry (see next chapter).

Brush the pastry with a little milk, make a small hole in the top with the point of a knife, and bake in the oven until the pastry is brown and crispy.

end, roll it over once, tuck in the ends like a parcel, then continue rolling towards the pointed end. The tip can be sealed with a little water if you wish.

The pie recipe *can be made with pork or beef (use less milk and more stock/gravy). For a more solid pie you can line the base with pastry before putting in the filling.*

Lamb *does not reheat very well, but is delicious cold. Serve plenty of it with redcurrant jelly and a baked jacket potato.*

CHAPTER 6:   SOMETHING OUT OF NOTHING

The Cyclades are barren islands although there is a particular majesty about them. Like an unclothed lady baring her breasts with dignity, the mountain tops that are now only islands, point their tips to the sky, swathed in a mantle of sea-blue silk. Bill Baggy avoided the busy resorts and tacked his sailing boat amongst the smaller islands where white-walled towns clung to the steep hillsides reflecting the heat of the summer sun.

It had been a long time since he had visited a supermarket and supplies were often hard to come by. There had been times when all he had was a few potatoes and onions; perhaps an egg or two. Several times in the evening calm he had climbed interminable steps from the shore-side in search of a shop, only to return with no more than a packet of biscuits and a tin of condensed milk. The black-spotted tomatoes and green-sprouting onions he left where they were, and wondered yet again at the reluctance of the locals to cultivate even a small patch of their barren lands. Surely there would be a place for a few 'scratchers' and a potato plot sheltered from the searing *katabatik* winds behind a stone wall or a hedge of thorn bushes?

At the very top of one village, after asking directions several times, he found a butcher's shop with a very modern refrigerator and a butcher's block made in the traditional way from the bole of a yew tree. Baggy reflected that into this ancient bole a thousand carcasses may have shed their blood! The point of a meat-cleaver was stuck in it, at the ready. He asked the butcher for two pork chops, knowing it was the most available meat in these parts and sure enough the EU-stamped carcass was duly cleaved on the yew tree-bole. Baggy watched with some trepidation as the ash threatened to fall from the butcher's drooping cigarette clasped firmly between his lips. The butcher too must have sensed the danger, for he carefully unstuck it from his lips and pressed it with yellowed fingers into the rest of the dog-ends in the ashtray at his side. Baggy declined the offer of some grey-coloured minced beef and made his way back down the hillside, pleased with his little package of meat in spite of everything.

Along the way he noticed a deserted apple tree shedding its ripe fruit on the ground. Only the wasps were taking any notice of the neglected harvest so he carefully picked up a few of the apples and popped them in his bag. At least he would dine well tonight on pork chops and apple rings. It would make a change from his many 'make-do' meals when he had to create something out of virtually nothing in his store cupboard.

The sinking sun was setting the landscape afire with vibrant colours as he descended the steep stony path. As he reached the bay with his boat waiting patiently for him he suddenly felt totally at peace with it all. Nothing seemed important. It was a different world and he was happy to be in it.

RECIPES

Grandma Baggywrinkle's Cornish Pasties ☐

Utensils

Floured board and rolling pin (see T & T)
Mixing bowl for pastry
Bowl for meat mixture
Baking sheet or roasting tray
Oven, pre-heated to gas mk. 6

Ingredients (to make 4 - 6 pasties)

For the filling:

1 large potato, peeled and diced
1 carrot or piece of swede, peeled and coarsely grated
1 onion, chopped finely
½ lb (250 g) cooked beef, diced
½ tsp oregano or mixed herbs
Plenty of salt and freshly ground black pepper
A little left-over gravy if you have it, or 1 tbsp oil

For the pastry:

One 12 oz (336 g) packet of ready-made pastry, OR:

4 oz (110 g) plain flour
4 oz (110 g) self-raising flour
4 oz (110 g) margarine (or half marg.,

TIPS & TECHNIQUES

If you decide to have a go at making pastry for the pasties rather than using a ready-made packet, it is a very good recipe on which to practice because pasty-pastry is traditionally pretty solid, and you don't need to bother with lining a dish. Also the pieces you are working with are relatively small and manageable.

A Rolling Pin *with handles on the end is unmanageable in a small working area. Baggy sawed the ends off his, since he deemed them unnecessary anyway.*

If you do not have a rolling pin, a small bottle or a beer can (a full one) will do the job just as well. (Don't forget later to allow the beer to settle before opening it up!)

Pasties *were originally made of whatever was to hand, wrapped up in a fairly solid bit of pastry for the men to take to the fields with them for their lunch. Poor folk would fill them with swedes and parsley moistened perhaps with a little clotted cream from the house cow.*

The thick bit of pastry, where it is folded over in the making, was for the workman to hold it with when his hands were dirty; then that bit of

half lard or suet)
½ cup of cold water
A little beaten egg or milk

Method

1. Mix all the ingredients for the filling together and leave it to stand.

2. Make the pastry by breaking up the fat amongst the flour with your fingers. Add the water and form it into a lump that holds nicely together. It should leave the bowl clean.

3. Divide it into 4 – 6 equal pieces.

4. Roll one piece out on a floured board, making sure there is enough flour on top of the pastry as well as underneath to prevent it sticking. Put a little flour on the baking tray as well. Your pastry should make a round approx. 6" (15 cms) in diameter.

5. Put a heaped tablespoon or more of the filling onto the middle of the pastry. Moisten the edges with the egg mixture or milk. Now fold one edge over the other and press them together to form a sealed packet. Lift the pasty lightly but firmly and place it on the baking sheet.

6. Continue making the rest of the pasties in the same way. Coat each one with the milk/egg mixture.

pastry was thrown to the dog.

Although this pasty recipe is with cooked meat, it is traditionally made with raw minced meat. In this case, omit the gravy/oil, because the juices and fat from the uncooked meat permeate the vegetables. With cooked meat you need to replace what you took out when you cooked it before.

Instead of folding your pasties flat as per the recipe, you could place the filling in the centre of the round and pinch the sides together with the fold coming over the top, which looks nicer and holds the filling better.

Baggy rolled the pastry out to the size of his outstretched fingers and simply pressed the edges together with his thumb.

It is the milk/egg mixture that makes the pastry shiny, so although it seems a bother at the time, you realise it is worth it when you take the lovely golden pasties out of the oven.

A pastry brush should be used for this, but Baggy just used his fingers.

Don't bother with an extra bowl for the milk/egg mixture: just put it in the bowl in which you mixed the pastry.

***A flan** or pie is an excellent*

7. Bake the pasties in the oven, gas mk. 6 for 20 minutes then reduce the heat to mk. 4 (moderate) and cook for a further 30 minutes.

Potato & Onion Flan ☐

Utensils

2 saucepans or 1 saucepan & one frying pan
1 mixing bowl
1 flan dish 7"– 8" (18 - 20 cm)
Oven gas mk. 4

Ingredients

For the pastry:

2 oz (56g) plain flour
2 oz (56g) self-raising flour
2 oz (56g) butter or margarine
1 oz grated cheese
¼ cup cold water

(Or: ready-made frozen shortcrust pastry, de-frosted)

For the filling:

2 medium potatoes, peeled and cut in pieces the size of ½ an egg
2 onions, cut in rings
1 clove garlic, crushed
2 oz (50 g) butter

way of making food go further. It is a simple edible container for whatever you wish to put in it.

Self-raising flour *can be found in most grocery shops or supermarkets. It is plain flour with the raising agent already mixed in with it to the correct proportion for baking. However, for pastry it can be a bit too light, and Baggy found that half plain, half self-raising was best for his pastry.*

If you do not have self-raising flour you need to add a little soda-bicarbonate to your plain flour in the proportion of roughly ½ teaspoon to 4 oz (100 g) flour.

Making Pastry *- The important thing is to get the final mixture so that you can handle it without it breaking up. The following tips will help you to do this.*

Use a large, wide-mouthed bowl for mixing. If you do not have one you could use a small plastic washing-up bowl.

Any fat will do, or any mixture of fat, except for soft margarine as it is too oily. It is a lot easier if the fat is not straight from the fridge.

Have the water ready to hand in a cup or jug, and have a little extra

1 tbsp plain flour
½ pt (275 ml) milk
1 oz (28 g) grated cheese (optional)
Salt & pepper
1 tbsp fresh chopped parsley
1 egg, beaten

Method

1. Make the pastry by rubbing the fat into the flour in the mixing bowl. Add the water and form it into a ball. (See T & T).

2. Use an old butter wrapper to rub some fat round the flan dish. Roll out the pastry and line the flan dish. Prick the pastry with a fork or pointed knife and cover it firmly with the butter paper, buttery side down. Bake in the oven for 10 minutes, until the edges of the pastry are slightly puffy but not brown. Remove the paper.

3. Meanwhile, boil the potato pieces in some salted water for 10 minutes, drain, and spread them in the pastry case when it is ready.

4. In the other pan, braise the onion rings and garlic in the butter until the onion is transparent and just tinged with brown.

5. Sprinkle in the flour to take up the fat, stir in the milk and combine it to make a creamy sauce around the onion

just in case. Too much water can be rectified more easily than too little.

Pretend you are in a great hurry. It is better to have lumps of fat left in the mixture than to work it to death in order to have it fine and crumbly. The more you work it, the more the heat of your hands will spoil it.

When you pour the water in use your fingers like a mixing machine, gradually getting it all to stick together. If you still have crumbly dry bits, add more water rather than trying to make do with what you have. If you have added too much water, throw a bit of flour over it and carry on.

Always use plenty of flour on the rolling surface and on the rolling pin.

Weighing the ingredients for pastry is a nuisance, so look at the ingredients the first time you do it and see how far up the side of your bowl the flour comes.

What does it look like when the fat has been rubbed in? If you can remember that, you don't need to weigh the fat next time.

Remember you can always judge your fat by thinking of it as a proportion of the pack. The same

pieces. Add the parsley, salt and pepper.

6. Remove the pan from the heat and stir in the beaten egg. Pour over the potatoes in the pastry case, and sprinkle the cheese on top.

7. Bake in the oven for 20 – 30 minutes, until the top is brown.

Quiche Lorraine □ *

Utensils
1 large mixing bowl
1 flan dish 7 "– 8" (18 - 20 cm)
Oven gas mk. 4

Ingredients
One quantity of pastry: (as above)
(Or ready-made short crust pastry, defrosted)

For the filling:

Butter size of ½ an egg
2 rashers of bacon, chopped
½ onion, chopped
3 eggs
½ cup milk
1 oz (30g) grated cheese
A pinch of sage
1 tbsp fresh chopped parsley
Pepper and a little salt

applies to a bag of flour.

Next time: try it without measuring - you may find it is even better!

Always make sure you roll out enough pastry to fill the flan dish easily, pressing the pastry into the edges and not pulling it to make it fit. If you do, it will only shrink back to its original size or less when you bake it.

***For a flan** you first need to bake it 'blind' i.e. without its contents, so that the crust is firm when the rather liquid mixture goes into it. Not doing this can result in a soggy bottom!*

***For a tastier pastry** you can add cheese or herbs or mustard to the mix before adding the water.*

***If you have pastry bits left over**, make them into cheese or anchovy sticks or biscuits. These make excellent 'nibbles' to go with a drink.*

Roll them out into a round; spread half the round with cheese and spread the other half with garlic, mustard, chili sauce, or whatever you fancy. Fold one half over the other, roll out again and cut into squares or fingers and bake in the oven.

Baggy would sprinkle them

½ tomato, diced (for garnish)

Method

1. Make the flan case by following steps 1 & 2 above.

2. Meanwhile, fry the bacon and onion in the butter with the pepper and place them in the pastry case.

4. In the mixing bowl that you used for the pastry (no need to wash it) beat the eggs with the milk. Add the herbs and cheese, saving a little cheese for the top, then pour it into the pastry case over the bacon mixture. Sprinkle the chopped tomato on top and a final sprinkling of grated cheese.

5. Bake in the oven for 20 – 30 mins until it is firm to the touch and light brown on top.

Stuffed Cabbage Leaves □

Utensils
1 large saucepan
1 frying pan
1 casserole dish

Ingredients
4 outer leaves of a large cabbage
1 tomato
2 oz (56 g) rice

before baking with what he called his 'Tunisian Mix' – cumin seeds, sumac seeds and black pepper seeds – a mixture he had found for sprinkling on bread in Tunisia.

Potato & Onion Flan *can also be made very successfully with Leek. One large leek, carefully washed and prepared (see T & T p.10) will be sufficient + a little finely chopped onion.*

The addition of some grilled bacon pieces laid across the top instead of the cheese looks and tastes great.

A Quiche *is just a fancy name for a savoury flan. You can in fact put whatever ingredients you like into it, pour some egg over, and bake it. The addition of milk or cream to the egg prevents it from being too solid.*

Use a little of the egg filling to cover the edges of the pastry so that it turns a nice golden colour.

Mushrooms make a worthwhile addition to a quiche, as do sweetcorn and peas.

A variety of vegetables can be used in quiches, or savoury flans, such as spinach, artichoke hearts or asparagus.

Whatever you use they always

Olive oil
Chopped bacon
½ onion, finely chopped
1 clove garlic, crushed
2 oz (56 g) cashew nuts
1 oz (28 g) sultanas
1 tbsp parsley
1 tbsp fresh basil leaves, chopped OR 1 tbsp pesto sauce
I pkt. celery cup-a-soup mixed thick
A few breadcrumbs
Parmesan cheese

Method

1. Bring a large pan of salted water to the boil.

2. Meanwhile, prepare the cabbage leaves by carefully peeling six individual whole leaves from the cabbage. Halve them by removing the stem. Blanch them for 2 minutes in the boiling water. Remove them to a plate or bowl of cold water.

3. Dunk the tomato in the same boiling water then remove the skin with a sharp pointed knife, and cut it into small pieces.

4. Now throw the rice into the boiling water and cook for 10 minutes.

5. Meanwhile, fry the bacon, onion and garlic in a little olive oil; add the tomato pieces, cashew nuts, sultanas, pesto

seem to look good and taste wonderful. A flan can be eaten hot or cold. It will keep well in a fridge and heat up easily in a microwave or oven.

They are the ideal picnic dish, lunchtime snack, party food, or even as a starter on a dinner menu when individual little flans can be served instead of a slice.

The Stuffed Cabbage recipe *is based on a Greek or Turkish recipe for Dolmades but baked in an oven with a sauce.*

Dolmades *is a traditional Mediterranean dish of vine leaves stuffed with a tasty rice filling. Like so many 'peasant' dishes it can be less than exciting since it evolved out of using basics that were to hand, but it can be equally delicious if well-made with good ingredients.*

So, if you can stuff vine leaves you can certainly stuff cabbage leaves, and in fact they are much easier to handle. They are tasty, and they use up the outside leaves that would otherwise be thrown away. It is also a healthy option.

It is your decision to stuff them with whatever you think would improve this recipe – or whatever you have to hand at the time.

sauce, parsley and finally the rice.

6. Place half the condensed soup in the casserole dish.

7. Wrap a spoonful of the filling in each cabbage leaf and place it in the casserole dish.

8. Finally pour the remaining soup mixture over the stuffed cabbage leaves; sprinkle it with breadcrumbs and parmesan cheese.

9. Bake for 20 – 30 minutes in the oven, gas mk. 5

Bread & Butter Savoury Pudding ✓

Utensils
I ovenproof dish
1 bowl for eggs
Oven at medium heat

Ingredients
Slices of stale (or fresh) bread
Butter or margarine
3 - 4 oz (100 g) grated cheese
Diced tomato, onion and/or any leftover cooked vegetables (peas, beans etc.)
Fresh parsley or coriander or Fine Herbes
4 Eggs beaten with ½ - ¾ pt (10-15 fl oz) milk, salt, pepper and mustard

You can stuff almost anything with almost anything!

If you don't have a cup-a-soup, mix part of any packet soup to the thickness of a cream sauce rather than a soup.

A spoonful of Crème Fraise or fresh cream added to the soup-mixture makes a world of difference.

The savoury bread pudding was a favourite Baggy remembered from his childhood. It was a standby of his mother's when the weekly housekeeping had run out.

It can also be made with filo or borek pastry. Put two whole rounds into the dish first and bring it over the top when the dish is full, like a parcel. Brush with butter between each layer of pastry.

Don't be tempted to think it is cooked when it looks a bit brown on top. For the inside to be cooked it needs to have risen up like a soufflé before you take it out of the oven.

Thin slices of cheese will do just as well if you can't be bothered to grate it.

The bread and butter pudding can be made up a day in advance and cooked when required.

Method

1. Butter the bread on one side and line your bowl with it, bottom and sides, with the buttered side against the dish.

2. Scatter some of the ingredients over the bread including some cheese then cover it with more bread and another layer of ingredients, saving a little cheese for the top.

3. Continue layering in this way. Cut the final piece of bread into smaller pieces and place them butter side up on top with the last of the cheese.

4. Pour the egg mixture over it all and press the bread down with your hands so that it absorbs the egg mixture. Add more milk if necessary.

5. Bake in a medium oven until the top rises up into a dome and the topping is brown.

Chopped up pieces of ham, sausage or bacon make a welcome addition.

Sage *goes well with both egg and cheese. It grows well in a garden or can be found growing wild in Mediterranean countries. It has a strong taste, so use it gently at first.*

The traditional sweet version of the Bread Pudding is made in exactly the same way but with currants and sultanas, bits of apple or whatever is to hand, instead of the cheese and vegetable; and with some sugar and cinnamon spice added to the milk and egg.

CHAPTER 7: TOO MANY MACKERELL

One deceptively bright calm morning Baggy set sail only to find by lunchtime that he was thrashing along in a hooley. He had already rolled up half the foresail and put a reef in the mainsail, but still the leeward deck of *The Sea Crow* was skimming the water and a white wake swooshed behind him. A barren island lay off to starboard so he altered course towards it, and soon ducked into a deserted bay that afforded surprisingly good shelter at the end of its dogleg. He was quite tired by the time the sails were furled and the anchor was down. There was not a soul around. Only the tinkling of goat bells broke the silence. He poured himself a soporific glass of wine, ate a quick 'Omelette Fine Herbes' and crept thankfully into his bunk for a comforting siesta.

It was mid-afternoon when he was suddenly aroused by the sound of heavy engines thundering past and something landing with a thud in the cockpit. Bleary-eyed he peered out, to find he was surrounded in his so called deserted bay by half a dozen large and brightly painted fishing boats, which presumably also had ducked out of the *meltemi* which was now blowing strongly outside.

The thud he had heard had come from a large mackerel, which was just giving a desultory gasp of expiration in the cockpit. He was gazing at it in surprise when another fishing boat came past with cheery fishermen aboard who seemed amazed to see him there and bombarded him with laughter and another half-dozen mackerel. It was raining mackerel! He waved and hollered a "thank you!" but only a churning white wake answered him.

"Now what on earth do I do with this lot?" he said, scratching his head but unable to suppress a grin of delight.

He gutted them in a bucket of sea water in the cockpit to the cheers (or was it jeers?) of a flock of seagulls, and soon had five of the fine fish in a large frying pan foaming with butter, their tails forming a fan around the edge. He lifted a tail and hoped - beyond hope - that it would not stick to the pan, so dropped it back again when it did.

"But this is too simple for such beautiful fish," he remarked to himself. He cut some onion finely, sprinkled it in the pan together with some garlic and parsley then, when he managed to turn the fish over, gave them a generous splash of ouzo and sizzled it all about with a shake of the pan over a high heat and for good measure added some of his home-pickled capers.

He dined in style that night with no addition to the fish except a wedge of lemon, crisp lettuce and crusty bread.

Next morning when he looked at the remains in the pan, he discovered that the liquid had formed a delicious jelly around the fish, which he knew would preserve them for another meal.

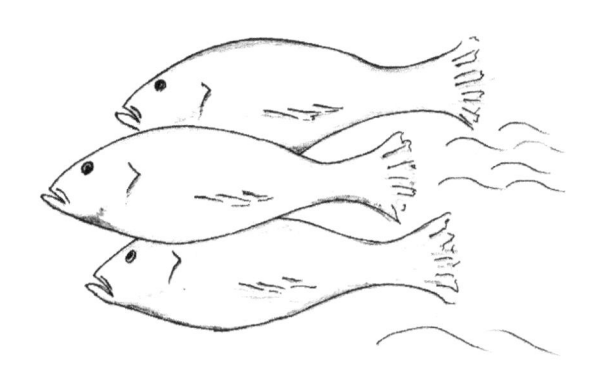

RECIPES

Mackerel Fried with Ouzo ✓ ☐

<u>Utensils</u>
1 large frying pan
1 gas ring

<u>Ingredients</u>
1 mackerel per person
½ onion, finely chopped
1 oz (25g) butter
A dash of ouzo, pernod or similar aniseed liquor
Salt & freshly ground black pepper
Fresh parsley
Wedge of lemon

<u>Method</u>

1. Melt some butter in a large frying pan; place the mackerel in it followed by the onion. Add the salt and pepper.

2. Cook for 5 minutes, adjusting the heat so that it does not burn the skin but just sizzles away. Cover with a lid or tin foil.

3. Turn the fish over carefully and splash in the ouzo. Sprinkle on half the parsley and simmer slowly for 5 - 8 minutes, basting any liquid over the fish.

TIPS & TECHNIQUES

Gutting fish. If you follow Baggy's simple instructions this will not be as awful and messy as many people make it. He had it down to a fine set of rules that applied whether the fish was the size of a sardine or a tuna.

1) Hold the fish by the head between finger and thumb of one hand. Cut down from the back of the head behind the gills, but stop just before you are all the way through.

2) Now put down your knife and take hold of the fish with both hands. Pull the head down and away from the body and you will find that the innards also come away attached to the head.

3) Any remaining gunge will wash away under a tap or in a bucket of water.

Sardines do not have to be prepared in this way but can be cooked with their heads and tails on. The head makes a convenient holding place when eating them in your fingers. Some people eat the heads and tails as well.

Fish Bones. Little fish like anchovies and sardines, which remain

4. Squeeze a wedge of lemon over the fish and sprinkle with the remaining parsley.

Serve with fresh crusty bread and salad.

Greek Sardines (fried in garlic) ✓

Utensils
1 large frying pan

Ingredients
6 - 8 sardines per person
1 clove of garlic, crushed
Plain flour
Olive oil
Salt & freshly ground black pepper
Parsley
Wedge of lemon

Method

1. Mix the flour with the salt and pepper and crushed garlic and coat each fish with it. Alternatively, put the flour and seasoning in a polythene bag, add the fish 4 - 5 at a time and shake.

2. Heat the oil in the frying pan, add the fish and fry until the underside is brown.

3. Turn the fish and fry again until cooked.

small when adult, have a bone structure that is proportionately easy to cope with. A simple backbone with ribs is easily removed attached to the head, and any smaller bones are so tiny they are hardly noticed.

Nowadays however, fishermen will take and sell whatever is in their nets, hence one will find in fishmongers' shops many baby fish that may resemble sardines or look ideal for the recipe opposite, but when you come to eat them will be just a mass of horrible bones.

This is because the bone structure is formed for a large fish but in the juvenile state these bones are short, spiky and often too small to find. They can turn a promising meal into an unpleasant battle.

I would discourage anyone from eating them for this reason alone but would in any case avoid these baby fish on principle.

'Sardines' used to be the traditional Mediterranean fisherman's fare in the days when his dinner consisted of the 'small fry' that no one wanted to buy. These days there is often little else but 'small fry' to buy.

The aniseed flavoured aperitif *we know as Pastis in France, Pernod in Italy, Ouzo in Greece and*

4. Turn off the heat and squeeze lemon over the fish, sprinkle with parsley and serve from the pan with chunks of fresh, crusty bread.

Anchovies ✓
- fresh ones of course –

<u>Utensils</u>
Clean plastic bag
Frying pan

<u>Ingredients</u>
12 anchovies per person
1 clove garlic, crushed
Plain flour
Olive oil
Salt & pepper
Parsley, chopped
Wedge of lemon

<u>Method</u>

1. Fillet the anchovies if required (see T & T)

2. Put the flour, seasoning and garlic in a plastic bag. Add the fish and shake well.

3. Heat the oil in the frying pan, add the fish and fry until cooked, stirring them about so they are cooked on all sides.

Rakı in Turkey is an excellent addition to any of the oilier fish like mackerel and fresh tuna. It compensates the oiliness of the fish and helps to preserve it too.

As with all flavourings it should be used judiciously so that you are not really aware of the taste of aniseed but it simply enhances the flavour of the fish.

The Scandinavians traditionally use the anise-flavoured herb dill in their fish dishes.

Anchovies: *when these tiny fish are in season they are really cheap and delicious. But be careful they are not caught in polluted water. Baggy would not eat the ones from the Black Sea, knowing the heavy metals accumulated in the water there would be absorbed by the fish.*

Boning anchovies could not be simpler. Take the head of the fish between finger and thumb of your left hand and hold the fish by the 'shoulders' in your right hand.

Pull one away from the other, and the head and backbone together with the rib-cage will come away, leaving the filleted fish in your right hand. You may need to just pinch it above the tail to remove the body from the bones with the tail attached. If the anchovies are not fresh, the flesh will

4. Turn off the heat and squeeze lemon over the fish, sprinkle with parsley and serve from the pan with chunks of fresh, crusty bread.

Baked Salmon with Parsley or Dill Sauce ☐ *

(Serves 4 people)

Utensils
Casserole dish or baking tray
Small saucepan
Strainer
Oven
1 gas ring

Ingredients
A chunk of salmon approx. 6"- 8" (20 cm)
Boiling water
½ cup if white wine
½ onion cut in rings
A stick of celery, chopped
Salt
6 whole peppercorns
A bay leaf
A small bunch of fresh parsley or dill
A little butter

Method

1. Put a little boiling water in the bottom of the casserole dish. Place the fish in it and add the onion rings,

break up and/or stick to the bones. When dealing with small fish, even more than with anything else, the freshness of the produce is vital.

Boning a cooked fish *successfully is very simple once you have understood the basic anatomy, which applies to all vertebrates. A backbone runs down the middle, attached to the head and tail at each end, with ribs and side bones coming off it.*

(Do not try this with uncooked fish as it is very much more difficult).

1) Take a sharp, wide-bladed knife and cut the fish down the back so that all the upward-pointing bones are on the same side of your knife.

2) Lift the flesh away from the backbone with the help of the knife and remove it to the side of the plate or to another plate.

3) Take hold of the tail and lift the backbone away from the flesh all in one piece with as many side bones as possible attached to it.

4) The fins and the small bones attaching to them can be lifted away with the flat of the knife.

To choose a fresh fish *look at the eye. This is easy to do without the fishmonger even knowing which fish*

celery, salt, peppercorns and herbs. If you are using the head end of the fish, place the herbs inside the gullet. Smear the top with butter; pour the wine over it, then top up with more water if necessary to come half way up the fish.

2. Cover with a lid or tin foil and cook in a moderate oven for ½ hour turning the fish over once during the cooking time. (If you have room, it could also be cooked on the top plate).

3. Remove the fish from the liquid and cut it to remove the backbone and any other large bones. Turn off the oven and replace the fish in it to keep warm, wrapped in tin foil.

To make the sauce:

1. Strain the liquid into a small saucepan and boil it rapidly to reduce the quantity.

2. Chop the parsley finely.

3. Put a dessertspoonful of flour into a cup with a very little milk to make a creamy paste without any lumps. Pour it into the reduced liquid, stirring all the time.

4. Add the chopped parsley and cook gently, stirring for 2 minutes.

5. Pour over the fish and serve with

you are looking at. How long is it since that eye could see? If it looks glazed and cloudy, forget it. If it still has an alert look, examine further.

Lift the edge of the gill to see if the blood capillaries are still red.

The simplest test of all is to see whether the flesh is firm or soft. If possible, place a finger on the side of the fish as it lies on the slab. If your finger makes an indent, the fish is old.

Decay is what you are testing for, and don't forget it! So, don't be shy, and take no notice of the brusque attitude of fishmongers. The more they shout usually the worse their wares, and at the end of the day they will admire you for your judgment. Fishmongers and butchers can be some of the worst swindlers, but they will admire you if they realise you know what is what.

Many fish are now farmed rather than being caught in their natural environment. Fish farming suffers with the same problems as animal factory farming: mainly overcrowding which can lead to disease and inevitable medication, and nutrients that do not have the variety of the wild.

Farmed fish is easy to discern because it will be slimy to the touch. This makes the gutting described

mashed potato and a 'gentle' vegetable like peas, fennel bulb or artichokes.

Fishmonger's Pie ☐ *
(Serves 4 people)

Utensils
1 small saucepan
1 large saucepan
1 ovenproof pie dish or casserole dish
1 - 2 gas rings
Oven pre-heated to gas mk. 5

Ingredients
1 lb (450 g) white fish, or a variety of white fish/salmon/smoked fish
4 oz (110 g) prawns or any other shellfish
1 spring onion, finely chopped
2 pink-gilled mushrooms, finely chopped (optional)
1 lb (450 g) potatoes
2 hardboiled eggs, shelled and quartered
A little extra milk and butter for the potatoes
A tin of anchovies or a little cheese (optional)

Sauce made from:
1 oz (28 g) butter or margarine
½ pt (275 ml) milk
1 tbsp parsley or green coriander
Salt and pepper
A splash of sherry or anise liqueur

above difficult since it is hard to get a grip on the body or head of the fish.

After cooking fish in your all-purpose frying pan, you may want to get rid of the lingering fishy smell. Rubbing a wedge of lemon round it will do this very effectively.

In fact you may as well use the squeezed wedges of lemon you have been using for the fish - they will do quite well enough. You can also freshen your fingers with the lemon wedges then put them in the washing-up water.

Fennel Bulb is a wonderful vegetable to serve with fish. The anise aroma that comes as you cook it is not at all over-powering when you eat it. Boil it and serve it simply with a little melted butter or a white sauce.

Pepper - freshly ground black pepper is recommended for most of the dishes in this book. The pre-ground pepper looses the aromatic quality of the freshly ground berry, though some mild fish dishes are better enhanced by white ground pepper. Best of all is freshly ground mixed peppers (red, black and white).

Coriander leaves are an excellent accompaniment to fish. They have a very individual flavour so use them sparingly at first. As with all herbs, it should be hard to tell that

Method

1. Peel the potatoes, cut them into pieces the size of an egg, and boil them in a pan of water.

2. Place the raw fish in the casserole dish and sprinkle the shelled prawns or shellfish over it, together with the finely chopped onion and mushroom.

3. Make the parsley sauce by melting the butter or margarine in a small pan, adding the flour to absorb the butter then slowly adding the milk, stirring all the time until it makes a creamy sauce. Add the salt, pepper and parsley. Simmer for 1 minute.

4. Pour the sauce over the fish and replace it in the oven.

5. Test that the potatoes are cooked by putting a knife into one. It should be soft all the way through but not falling to pieces. Mash the potatoes, adding extra milk, butter or margarine, salt and pepper.

6. Take the fish from the oven and spread the potato on top, making little peaks with the fork in a nice pattern.

7. The top can be garnished with anchovies or with a little grated cheese.

8. Cook in the oven at gas mk. 4 for 30 they are even there, but it is an almost addictive flavour once you get to know it.

Fishmonger's Pie should ideally be made with a mixture of fish, and mixed pieces for a pie may be bought from a fishmonger. It is usually white fish, for this is a northern dish rather than a Mediterranean dish, and salmon is a happy addition. Seafood additions can be made up of broken pieces.

Potatoes, creamed or mashed, are one of the nicest accompaniments to fish and seafood. A potato masher is a great help, but finish off with a fork for a lighter texture and to get rid of any small lumps. Don't be mean with the milk and always add more salt and pepper.

'Creamed' is really just a fancy name for 'mashed', but if you wish you can add a dollop of cream as well.

There are so many different types of potato that to give exact cooking times is difficult. Some potatoes are waxy and yellow and take longer to cook; others are white and floury and easily fall apart in the cooking, especially if cut in half.

Large, 'old' potatoes (as opposed to small 'new' ones) can go into cold water and be brought to the

– 40 minutes by which time the fish should be cooked and the potato nicely brown on top.

Mild Fish Curry with Coconut ✓ ☐ *

Utensils
A large saucepan or slow cooker

Ingredients
1lb (500 g) white fish or fresh tuna meat
A handful of prawns or other seafood (optional)
Oil
1 onion, chopped
1 clove garlic, crushed
½ red or green pepper, chopped
1 tbsp curry powder
½ pt. coconut milk or 1 tbs. desiccated coconut mixed with milk or water or fish stock.
Salt
1 Star Anise
Chilli powder (if required)

Method

1. Heat the oil in the pan and fry the onion, pepper and garlic until soft.

2. Take the oil up with the curry powder and cook gently. Add the coconut milk to make a smooth cream. If it is too thick add a little more liquid.

boil with the water. This way they are less likely to fall apart. Large floury potatoes are best for mashing.

The curry recipe opposite is mild and aromatic so it brings out the flavour of the fish without overpowering it. The coconut and star anise are essential ingredients.

Coconut milk *is very useful for anyone suffering from an intolerance or allergy to dairy produce and can be used in almost any recipe where dairy milk is required.*

Star Anise *can be purchased in most supermarkets now. It is a beautiful star-shape and imparts a lovely aromatic flavour.*

This curry dish can be stretched with the addition of some boiled potatoes and/or hard-boiled eggs.

Ideally one should make one's own curry powder and vary it depending on the ingredients to be curried. But that needs another whole cookery book to itself. For Baggy's requirements an all-purpose curry powder was quite good enough.

The Slow Cooker *is ideal for curries, especially if the meat is quite tough, because it allows long slow cooking. The fish curry opposite can easily be done on the top of the stove*

3. Add the fish (and prawns if using them) and other ingredients. Cook gently until the ingredients have blended. Adjust seasoning if necessary.

Serve with rice, peas and a sliced banana.

as the fish cooks quite quickly, but it can equally be done in a slow cooker.

CHAPTER 8: UP THE CREEK

One day Bill Baggy found himself in the back of beyond. Having anchored up some nameless creek and been gale-bound for three days, he was starting to get rather lonely and hungry. He decided to set out in search of food, or at least in search of some form of habitation and companionship.

After tramping inland for three miles with an empty gas bottle in one hand and an empty wine flagon in the other, he came across a village with a few shops, all of which were surprisingly pertinent to his requirements. It seemed to be miles from anywhere but a winding stony road out of the village must have led to a larger settlement on the other side of the hills.

A small barefoot boy took charge of him, encouraging him along the dusty street to a tiny shop where he left his gas bottle for later collection and to another where he replenished his wine flagon.

"All human beings have the same basic needs," he reflected.

The butcher's shop, however, had a sad array of sheep's heads, chickens' gizzards, a rabbit hanging from a hook by a hind leg and the rump of a large ox hanging beside the door. Baggy indicated he would buy a piece of the large animal hanging by the door at which the grizzled butcher handed him a knife, indicating he should take what he wanted. Somewhat tentatively Baggy cut off a chunk and handed it to the butcher for wrapping, but before he could stop him the butcher had slapped it into a grinder and reduced it to a fine mince. It was not what Baggy had had in mind, but at his remonstrance the butcher indicated that without the mincing treatment he would not be able to get the meat past his teeth. At an exorbitant price he purchased the rabbit and at a surprisingly cheap price a handful of chicken offal. It must have been more meat than the butcher normally sold in a week.

With his packages safely wrapped in newspaper in his knapsack, he made his way to the local taverna where he drank strong coffee and rough cognac with a few elderly locals on hard-backed wooden chairs in the sunshine. Tourists were rarely seen in this village but his presence caused only polite interest.

At last, feeling refreshed in body and soul, with his rucksack slung over his shoulder, he made his way back over carpets of wild flowers and through hedges of scented myrtle to his boat in the placid creek.

On opening his packet from the shop he discovered amongst the gizzards a quantity of fresh chicken livers, which would have cost a lot of money back home. He put all the nasty-looking bits in his fish-trap, fried the chicken livers in butter and then sloshed them over with some of the cheap cognac he had purchased in the village. He thought they would make an excellent pâté for his lunches but was overtaken by the temptation to simply pop them in his mouth and wipe the juices from the pan with his fresh village-baked bread.

RECIPES

Baggy's Bolognaise Sauce ✓ ☐

Utensils
Deep frying pan or wide saucepan
1 gas ring

Ingredients
½ onion, finely chopped
½ pepper, green or red, finely chopped
3 mushrooms, chopped
1 clove garlic
Olive oil
4 oz (110 g) minced beef
1 small tin tomatoes
A pinch each of cumin, cinnamon & paprika
½ tsp oregano and/or thyme or mixed herbs
Salt & pepper

Method

1. Heat the oil in a deep frying pan; add the chopped onion and pepper. Cook until the onion just starts to brown then add the mushrooms and garlic. Fry for 3 minutes more.

2. Add the mincemeat, herbs, spices, salt and pepper, stirring well.

3. Stir in the tomatoes. Allow to bubble gently for 10 minutes.

TIPS & TECHNIQUES

The idea behind this chapter is that some dishes taste a lot better when the ingredients have had time to blend. This applies particularly to recipes that contain herbs or spices.

These recipes are also helpful if meat needs to be kept and space in the refrigerator is limited.

Before the days of refrigeration, *the addition of spices to meat was the primary method of preserving it, especially in hot countries.*

This is why curry is the prime ingredient in India. Chilies in South America do the same.

Spices *improve the flavour of slightly old meat and have a mildly antiseptic effect.*

Alcohol, yoghurt, garlic and herbs *all help to preserve meat.*

On a boat or in any situation where space in the refrigerator is at a premium, it may be useful to marinate meat in a spicy mixture, which would help keep it at least an extra day before cooking, as well as improving the flavour.

4. Cover the pan and remove it from the heat until needed; or continue cooking on as low a heat as possible for 15 - 20 mins.

For Spaghetti:

Bring to the boil a large pan of water, add the spaghetti and simmer until just soft. (About 10 mins). Drain the spaghetti and 'air' it. (See T & T). Re-heat the sauce if necessary and pour it over the spaghetti. Top with a sprinkle of grated Parmesan cheese.

Baggy's Beefburgers ✓ ☐

Utensils
A large mixing bowl
Frying pan

Ingredients
6 oz (180g) minced beef
¼ finely chopped onion
½ clove garlic, finely chopped
Salt & pepper
½ tsp oregano and/or thyme
A large pinch each of cumin, cinnamon and paprika
2 oz (56 g) white breadcrumbs
1 small egg, beaten
A little flour
Oil for frying

These marinades can also improve the flavour of bland mass-produced meat.

It may seem a nuisance to make a marinade and then have to leave the food until the next day before cooking. The answer is to think ahead and do the marinating when you buy the meat, then it is all ready when you want to cook it.

Minced meat *does not last well even in a fridge, so if you are worried about it going off before you can get round to using it, make it into this bolognaise sauce or the beefburger mix. The herbs and spices will help to preserve it, whilst the cooking will have killed off any lurking bacteria.*

Make sure the onions are really finely chopped; otherwise you will get bits sticking out of the beefburgers when you try to form them into rounds.

When frying beef-burgers*, fish, aubergine - or anything - try to turn them once only, or you will break them up and leave lots of bits in the pan. Don't poke, prod and worry them. If you see the underside is not done when you lift a corner and peer underneath: put it down again, and wait!*

The difference between herbs and spices: *herbs are green*

Method

1. Mix all the ingredients really well in a bowl, using your hands at the end for a good combination, adding just enough egg mixture to bind it. At this point the mixture can be kept for 1 or 2 days if necessary, and is certainly improved with keeping overnight in a refrigerator.

2. Put some flour or dry breadcrumbs (see T & T p. 37) on a board or plate. Divide the mixture into 4 parts and form each part into a ball; pat it flat on the crumbed or floured board, forming a beef-burger about ¾" (2 cms) thick.

3. Heat the oil in a frying pan and fry each side for 5 mins.

Chilli con Carne ✓ ☐

Utensils
1 medium saucepan

Ingredients
½ onion, chopped
1 clove garlic, crushed
4 oz (110g) minced beef
1 small tin tomatoes
1 tin of red kidney beans
½ tsp chilli powder or 1 chilli chopped and de-seeded
Salt & pepper

and come from the fresh leaves or flowers of the plant. Spices come from the root, seeds or stem of a plant; most usually grown in tropical areas, whereas herbs are more usual from the Mediterranean northwards. There are some exceptions, such as Saffron which is regarded as a spice but comes from the stamens of a specific Iris plant.

***Cinnamon**, a gentle spice, is the one that gives savoury dishes that specifically Mediterranean flavour that is so hard to recapture when you try to cook those holiday dishes back at home. Use just a pinch or a sprinkle until you get used to it. It is also good in puddings and cakes.*

***Cumin** is typical of middle-eastern dishes and should be used with caution until you grow accustomed to it. Just a little will turn a common dish into something exotic. In these dishes, a mere pinch will be enough - more will overpower the other flavours.*

***Paprika** is a spice that can be used in many dishes to give depth of flavour. Sweet paprika is mild and tasty, the hottest version is Chili powder. It is a spice that can vary from the 'sweet' Hungarian type to the very hot paprika that differs little from chili. So use it with caution until you know the strength of the paprika you have purchased.*

Method

1. Heat the oil in the saucepan and cook the onion and garlic until just turning brown. Add the mince and cook lightly.

2. Add the tomatoes, chilli and crumbled stock cube. Bring to simmering point and continue to cook for 10 minutes.

3. Add the red kidney beans and cook for a further 10 minutes. Leave it to mull until ready to eat. Reheat if necessary – improves with keeping.

Rabbit à la Moutarde ☐ *
(Serves 4 people)

Utensils
Frying pan
Small saucepan
Casserole dish
1 gas ring
Oven, gas mk. 3

Ingredients
1 rabbit cut in joints, excluding rib cage
Mustard, preferably Dijon
2 slices of fatty bacon, cut in pieces
1 onion
Flour
2 oz (56g) butter

It comes from the red and green peppers that we know so well and is a very useful addition to a number of dishes that just need a bit of 'oomph' to bring them out of the doldrums.

It can also be purchased in a very useful sauce called 'Harissa' packaged in a tube or jar.

Tabasco Sauce *does much the same thing but is considerably more refined.*

Chili*, as we all know, is very hot. The seeds and the vein to which they attach are the hottest part.*

Fresh red and green chilies can be purchased and, if you are in a dry climate, they can be hung up to dry for later use, if you wish. Take a needle and cotton and thread them through the stem-head, then hang them up where the air will get at them. They will turn a beautiful red and decorate the kitchen.

If you are only using part of a fresh chili, remember to cut it lengthways rather than across. That way the remainder will keep better. (See T & T p.116)

Anything cooked with chilies, as with curry powder, needs time on its side in order for the heat to

2 tbsp olive oil
Salt & pepper
Chicken stock cube
A splash of sherry
Fresh chopped parsley

Method

1. Spread the mustard over the rabbit and leave it to marinate overnight.

2. Coat the rabbit pieces with their mustard in seasoned flour and brown them in the butter and oil in a frying pan. Place them when done in the casserole dish.

3. Fry the bacon, onion and garlic until beginning to brown. Add it to the rabbit pieces including any oil in the pan.

4. Cover the casserole and cook in the oven, gas mk. 3 for ½ hour.

5. Meanwhile, mix the stock cube and cold water and any left-over flour in a small saucepan (or the frying pan you used before). Bring it to the boil while stirring. Add the sherry.

6. Add this to the casserole at the end of its ½ hour in the oven, and return it to the oven uncovered until brown on the top. Sprinkle with the parsley.

permeate the other flavours in the dish rather than simply overpower them.

Chili con Carne *is a good recipe for making ahead of schedule, and a good way of keeping the meat. The flavour certainly improves with keeping.*

We are accustomed nowadays to eating products containing a lot of thickening agents or glutinous substances so that an ordinary homemade sauce can seem a bit thin. Mix a heaped teaspoon of cornflour with cold water and add it to the simmering sauce. It will turn it cloudy at first, but soon clears when brought to the boil and gives it a shiny appearance.

Rabbit. *This is an unlucky word to mention on a boat. The reason is supposed to be because rabbits taken for food on the sailing ships of old had a way of gnawing at the wood, causing holes that could sink the ship!*

Rabbit is not popular meat in England these days, but in Europe it is bred in captivity for eating, and the flavour of it is really delicious. They are also much larger and tenderer than the traditional wild rabbit with its strong taste.

This rabbit recipe works very well in a Slow Cooker. In this case,

Bacon & Chicken Livers on Toast ✓∗

Utensils
Frying pan

Ingredients
4 chicken livers cut in pieces
2 rashers of bacon cut in pieces
A little butter
1 clove garlic, crushed
Black pepper

Method

1. Melt the butter in a frying pan; add the bacon pieces and crushed garlic. Fry until tinged with brown.

2. Add the prepared chicken livers and cook until firm, stirring and turning them in with the bacon pieces.

3. Add the black pepper and cognac. Raise the heat briefly.

This makes a gourmet snack, served on slices of toast. For a main meal, add it to some vegetable rice.

Chicken Liver Pâté ✓ ☐ ∗

Utensils
Frying pan
Liquidiser or blender (optional)

after stage 2 remove the meat to the slow cooker and add the other ingredients to it there.

Jointing a rabbit *is not anyone's idea of fun, but it really is not too difficult. If you are prepared to do it yourself you can make much better use of the available meat. Use a good sharp knife and a chopper to cut through the joints.*

The rib cage is the part that produces all the little bones that annoy and there is so little meat on it anyway, I suggest either not using it at all or only for making stock.

Mustard *is another spice useful for preserving and flavouring, with so many subtle varieties that put to shame the yellow stuff that goes on hot-dogs. To mention just a few:*

- English Mustard: bright yellow and hot as can be. It is good in mayonnaise, vinaigrette and mustard sauce. You can buy it ready made, or in powder form. The powder needs to be mixed with a little cold water. The advantage of buying the powder and mixing it as required is in the purity of flavour, but for convenience the ready-mixed is good enough.

- Dijon Mustard is a milder variety and preferable where a more subtle flavour is required. Best for the rabbit dish opposite, where it can be

Small glass bowls or ramekin dishes

Ingredients
1 lb (450g) chicken livers
Butter size of an egg
1 clove garlic
¼ tsp mixed spice
½ tsp mixed herbs
Salt & pepper
Small glass of sherry
Dash of brandy

Method

1. Cut the livers in half and remove any gristle. Cook them in the melted butter until firm but only just cooked. (2 - 3 minutes). As they are cooking, add the garlic, herbs and spices, salt and pepper.

2. Add alcohol, raising the heat and cooking very briefly.

3. Allow the livers to cool a little then either mash them with a fork or put them in a liquidiser so that any liquid is combined with the meat.

4. If you want to keep the pâté, put it in little dishes and pour melted butter over the top. The flavour of the pâté will improve with keeping.

used liberally; it is also good with some fish dishes. There are innumerable sub-varieties of Dijon mustard, as anyone who has visited that town will know.

- Whole Grain Mustard contains whole mustard seeds, whereas other mustards are made from the ground seeds. It also comes in a number of varieties and can make the eating of mustard a whole new experience. A spoonful mixed with the stock in the rabbit recipe gives the dish an extra tang.

Making pâté *is another very good way of preserving meat because the spices, herbs and alcohol prevent it from deteriorating. But bear in mind that nothing lasts for ever!*

Pâté is not something one generally thinks of making oneself, but this simple pâté is very quick and easy to do. Pâté goes a long way as a snack and is extremely tasty.

This pâté can be made with turkey or rabbit livers, but the taste is stronger and the texture is courser.

The melted butter on top of liver pâté keeps the air out and prevents it from discolouring.

CHAPTER 9: NIGHTWATCH

Sailing at night in the Mediterranean summer was a doddle even for a single-handed sailor. The wind invariably dropped and it was a case of motor-sailing on a calm sea beneath a cloudless star-filled sky with the autopilot doing the work. There was little for Baggy to do except to lie back in the cockpit and watch the constellations and planets in the vastness of the sky. It made him feel like a tiny speck bobbing on the ocean.

Sometimes the stars seemed to be the only solid thing in the vast ethereal blackness of the sky; at other times it was the sky that seemed solid, like a dark black lid with holes cut in it for the stars, where the light of some gigantic cosmic god shone through to him from the outside. But all this philosophising made Baggy inordinately hungry. He longed for something sweet – like a good hunk of old-fashioned fruitcake, jam tarts, or some of Mrs. B's chunky homemade shortbread.

In the middle of the night, for the first time Baggy sought out the recipe books again. It gave him a pretty good idea of how to make a fruit cake though as usual he wanted to give it his own additions. What he really needed was a cake that would not crumble in his hand between cake-tin and cockpit. Even with his appetite he reckoned a whole cake for one person would need to be of the kind that would keep for some time - like a Christmas or birthday cake.

Of course all this had to wait until the next day in harbour when he could concentrate on it, but straight away in the middle of the night he searched his store cupboard and found a surprising variety of dried fruit. There were raisins, sultanas, currants, dates and prunes - and hidden right at the back he found glacé cherries, candied peel and some old shelled walnuts. He also managed to dig out a rather dilapidated cake tin, which with great difficulty he lined with tinfoil to make it usable.

Into a large mixing bowl he tipped all the dry ingredients and mixed in the margarine with his fingers as best he could. For good measure he added a cereal bowl full of Albran and milk (because he had really wanted to use wholemeal flour). Brandy and sherry went in too, then he made a little well in the mixture and broke the eggs into it, beating them in to themselves first then mixing them into the rest of it, adding enough milk to make it somewhere between sticky and sloppy.

'Could this be dropping consistency?' he wondered.

The problem now was to get the oven low enough for it not to burn on the top and bottom before it was cooked in the middle, so he put a heatproof mat underneath it and some brown paper over the top, which helped. Eventually the cake felt quite firm when he patted it on the top so confirmed that it was done by putting a knife into it, which came out quite clean.

After his success with his Nightwatch Cake he decided he also needed something simpler as a stand-by and remembered the rock-buns of his childhood that old Ma Baggywrinkle used to bake. He would run off to school with a hot bun clasped in his hand, soon to be shovelled into his panting mouth. He liked this recipe particularly because he found he could do all the mixing and only get one hand floury while he steered the boat with the other, thus making it a useful occupation on an easy broad reach.

RECIPES

Nightwatch Cake ☐ ✻

Utensils
A large mixing bowl
A bowl to take the fruit
Cake tin 7 "- 8" (20 cm) diameter, or a large 'loaf' tin
Oven gas mk. 3

Ingredients
1lb (450g) dried fruit (any mixture of sultanas, raisins, currants, dates, and figs)
2 oz (56 g) glacé cherries
2 oz (56 g) walnuts, chopped (optional)
Candied peel, or a spoonful of marmalade
10oz (275 g) plain flour
2 oz (56 g) sugar
4 oz (110 g) margarine
Cereal bowl of Albran mixed with ½ pt (275 ml) milk
2 eggs
½ tsp allspice
A good splash of brandy

Method

1. Have your cake tin lined and ready (see T & T).

2. Wash the dried fruit and mix it with the nuts, spices and brandy in a bowl, having chopped up any large pieces

TIPS & TECHNIQUES

The very thought of lining a circular cake tin can put you off the whole idea of baking a cake. You can more easily use an oblong cake tin which will cook quicker too.

We used to have to line the rusty old tins with a layer of old butter or margarine wrappers in the bottom and up the sides, butter side up. But now you can buy special plastic-looking cake tins that will not melt away in the oven even though they look as if they would.

Baggy only had a rusty old round tin which he managed to line by placing the cake tin on some greaseproof paper and marking the diameter of it with a pencil. Then he cut a circle an inch larger all round, then cut notches between the outer circle and the inner one.

He fitted this paper into the bottom of the cake tin then cut a length of greaseproof paper long enough to go round the circumference of the tin and stand a little higher than the top of the tin, which he placed upright around the edge so that it sat within the bottom edge.

To test when a cake is cooked: *the traditional way is to put a skewer or knife into the middle of it*

(e.g. the dates). If you have time to leave it to stand, so much the better.

3. In a large mixing bowl combine the margarine and flour, as you would for making pastry.

4. Add the fruit mixture, the sugar and the Albran mixture. Stir it round and make a well in the centre. Break the eggs into this well and break them up with a fork, then gradually combine them with the rest of the ingredients.

5. Put the mixture into the lined cake tin, smooth the top level. Place over the top of it a butter wrapper and some thick brown paper with a hole made in the centre.

6. Place it in the centre of the pre-heated oven, gas mk. 3, or low down if your oven is small. Bake it for approx. 1 hour (long tin) or 2 hours (round tin).

Rock Buns ✓

Utensils
Mixing bowl
Baking tray sprinkled with flour
Oven, pre-heated to gas mk. 5

Ingredients
8 oz (225g) self-raising flour
1 egg, beaten lightly

and if it comes out clean, then the cake is cooked. But if the cake is not cooked this very action can cause it to sink in the middle. So before you do this, just lay your hand on the top. This way you can feel if it is worth testing with the knife or not.

Remember: if the knife comes out sticky, you must wash and dry it before you try again.

The paper over the top *of the cake is to prevent the top burning before the middle is cooked. It needs a hole in the top to allow steam to get out. Cut a round the size of the cake-tin, fold it in half, then half again and snip the pointed end off.*

If your oven is small, *turn the cake round during the cooking so that it cooks evenly on all sides.*

Cakes when cooked *should be removed from the tin or baking tray as soon as reasonably possible, and placed on a grill to cool.*

If this is not done the cake will tend to go hard on the bottom as it continues to cook from the heat of the tin.

Self-raising flour *makes life much simpler, even though proper chefs might not approve. It is simply plain flour already combined with baking powder, which is what makes*

2 oz (56g) lard or margarine
2 oz (56g) sugar
¼ tsp cinnamon
4 oz (110 g) sultanas, currants, or mixed dried fruit
¼ pt (150 ml) milk

Method

1. Rub the fat into the flour, (as for pastry). Add the sugar, fruit and spice.

2. Mix it well together; then combine it with the egg and just enough milk to make a very stiff mixture.

3. With the aid of two spoons put it in little heaps on the baking tray, remembering that they will increase in size with the cooking. This mixture should make 8 - 10 buns.

4. Bake in the oven gas mk. 5 for 10 minutes.

Scones ✓

Utensils
Mixing bowl
Baking tray sprinkled lightly with flour
Oven pre-heated to gas mk. 5

Ingredients
8 oz (225 g) self-raising flour
2 oz (56 g) margarine or lard

cakes rise when cooked.

If you have to use plain flour, add 1 teaspoon of baking powder to every 8 oz (225 g) of flour, or add the same amount of bicarbonate of soda and (if you have it) a pinch of Cream of Tartare.

A rubber spatula *is an extremely useful kitchen implement that costs very little. It is essential for scraping sticky mixtures out of the bottom of bowls and makes your washing up a lot easier too.*

Don't use it in a hot saucepan or the rubber may melt and blend with your food!

Save the wrappers *from packs of butter and margarine. They are always useful for greasing a pastry dish or a baking tray, or for lining a cake tin.*

Store them in a corner of the fridge so they do not go rancid, folded up in a jam jar.

Castor Sugar *is finer than granulated sugar and makes mixing for cake recipes easier. If you do not have it, granulated will do.*

Mixed Dried Fruit *can be purchased in supermarkets in England and is very useful to have in the store cupboard. It can be used in*

A pinch of salt
½ pt (275 ml) milk

Method

1. Rub the fat into the flour and salt in the mixing bowl.

2. Combine the milk with it and form it into a round about 1½" (3 cm) thick on a well-floured board.

3. Transfer the round to the baking sheet and cut it into six pieces, pulling them slightly apart from each other.

4. Bake in a pre-heated oven, gas mk. 5 for 10 minutes.

Flap Jacks ✓ ☐

Utensils
1 small saucepan
1 sandwich tin or small baking tray,
Oven pre-heated to gas mk. 5
1 gas ring

Ingredients
6 oz (170 g) porridge oats
1 oz (28 g) self-raising flour
2 - 3 tbsp (heaped) Golden Syrup
2 oz butter or margarine

any cake recipe where dried fruit is required and often makes a more interesting flavour than plain sultanas.

Mixed dried fruit also contains pieces of candied mixed peel. If your recipe specifically requires it and you do not have it, a spoonful of chunky marmalade will do instead.

Raisins are the largest mid-brown coloured dried fruit. They are the tastiest but often have seeds lurking in them, which is a nuisance. Sultanas are the large pale coloured ones, probably the most useful. Currants are small, dark and very tasty. All are dried grapes.

Cinnamon comes from the aromatic bark of a tropical tree and adds a pleasant spiciness to cakes and desserts.

Allspice gives a stronger spiciness to cakes. It has an aroma and taste of nutmeg, cloves, and cinnamon, though it is in fact a small dried berry in its own right.

Brandy in a cake will help to keep it from going moldy. A good rich fruitcake should keep well for some months either in a tin or wrapped in tinfoil.

You can if you wish, feed it with a little sherry or brandy now and

Method

1. In a small saucepan heat the golden syrup and fat.

2. Stir in the oats and flour.

3. Spread the mixture into the tin and bake in the pre-heated oven for 15 - 20 minutes.

4. Cut into sections with a sharp knife, but do not attempt to remove it from the tin until it is quite cold.

4 x 4 Sponge Cake *

Utensils

Large mixing bowl
Electric mixer or balloon whisk
Sieve
Rubber spatula (optional)
2 sandwich tins lined with butter papers or greaseproof paper. (See T & T)
Oven pre-heated to gas mk. 4

Ingredients
4 eggs
4 oz (110 g) white sugar, preferably castor sugar
4 oz (110 g) self-raising flour
Strawberry jam for filling and whipped cream (optional)

then which will also help to keep it moist. Make small holes in it with a skewer or prong so that the liqueur runs to the middle of the cake.

Flap Jacks keep well in a tin and taste better for keeping.

Golden Syrup is a peculiarly English concoction. It is one of those items that those who live abroad may find a space for in their luggage, knowing it cannot be bought in foreign parts.

Plain scones can be varied by adding a few sultanas and/or a little cinnamon to make them more interesting.

Scones are a wonderful substitute if you have run out of bread. They do not have to be sweet. You can omit the sugar and instead add some cheese and mustard to make a tasty savoury scone. Alternatively, put in some herbs and garlic. Just perfect to go with a bowl of soup.

Sponge Cake can be made in one deeper cake tin and then cut in half when cooked. This may be easier if you only have a small oven.

Although this is simpler at the start, it is not always easy to cut the sponge evenly especially if it has turned out beautifully light!

Method

1. Whisk the eggs and sugar until pale and fluffy - they should distinctly change colour. An electric mixer is best for this, but if you do not have one, a balloon whisk will do very well.

2. Sieve the flour into the mixture and combine it gently but quickly with a spoon or rubber spatula, which will also be useful for scraping the mixture out of the bowl.

3. Divide the mixture between two round sandwich tins and bake them at gas mk. 4 for 20 minutes or until firm to the touch and nicely risen.

4. Allow to cool out of the tins and sandwich them together with strawberry jam and cream. Sprinkle a little castor sugar or icing sugar on top.

For lining the tin, first lay it on the greaseproof paper and mark a line around the tin before cutting the paper..

This sponge cake is a healthy option since it contains no fat.

A simple sponge cake with a cream and jam filling is really delicious and redolent of Ye Olde English Tea Shoppe.

It also makes a good desert if topped with fruit. (See page 136)

CHAPTER 10: THE SQUIRREL INSTINCT

Baggy's cooking began to extend a little further than the mere provision of meals to keep body and soul together. On rainy days when he had time on his hands he could make all kinds of preserves to store away. He remembered how his mother would make marmalade and jams when there was a surfeit of fruit and now he often found he could pick up windfalls that nobody wanted and frequently came across trees that had gone wild in gardens long since gone to waste. It was only a question of sorting out a few basic recipes.

Herbs too could often be picked wild and he found they dried all by themselves if put out in the sun or hung in a warm airy place. Then when they were crisp and dry they could easily be crumbled finely and stored in a small jar.

Often he was not in a place where he could nip out to the supermarket for a jar of mayonnaise or a fizzy drink so he liked to have a good store in his 'bilge larder' where it kept nice and cool and away from flies and bugs. It was always a good idea too to have some stores for that unexpected guest; and when a small present was required he found a jar of his home-made jelly always went down well.

One day when he was anchored in a lonely bay another sailing yacht with a French flag dropped anchor not far from him. He noticed with surprise that the lone yachtsman who waved a cheery 'Bonjour' appeared to have only one leg though he managed to move around his yacht very well. Single-handed sailing was one thing but single-legged as well was something else! Baggy decided to invite his neighbour over for a sundowner – he knew it would not be an impossibility for he had seen the man lowering himself over the side of his boat into his dinghy. At the appointed time the Frenchman rowed across and clambered onto *The Sea Crow*. Baggy had put out on the table in the cockpit some olives, homemade cheese straws and a garlicky mayonnaise dip, for he knew that Frenchmen like a little something to go with a drink, thus turning 'a drink' into '*un aperitif*'.

Pierre sat himself comfortably down in the cockpit and immediately (rather rudely to Baggy's mind) dipped his finger in the mayonnaise and noisily sucked at it. "Aaah" he said, dipped and tasted again, then threw his arms in the air, put his head back and cried, "Aaaaolee!" Baggy wondered whether he should join in with a "Hooraaay" but the Frenchman continued, "Where did you find Aioli? It is wonderful – I have not tasted true Aioli since I left Corsica – where did you find this wonderful garlic sauce in this wild land?"

Baggy was rather shy about admitting to a total stranger that he had actually made it himself and as far as he was concerned it was just some of his homemade mayonnaise to which he usually added some garlic. But Pierre was appreciative of Baggy's culinary interests and they spent a happy couple of hours discussing recipes together, which made a change for both of them from the usual yachtsmen's talk of engine problems, toilet repairs and where to find spare parts.

RECIPES

Garlic Mayonnaise (Aioli) □ *

Utensils
1 large mixing bowl
1 small bowl (for egg whites)
Balloon whisk
Measuring jug for the oil
Jam jar or storage container

Ingredients
2 egg yolks + a little white
1 level tsp salt
½ pt (225 ml) sunflower oil
1 heaped tsp mustard
1-2 cloves of garlic, crushed
Fresh ground black pepper
Wine vinegar (preferably white) or lemon juice

Method

1. Take your two bowls and divide the egg yolks from the white, placing the yolks in the larger one and saving the white in the smaller. No need to be fussy if you leave some white in with the yolks. Add the salt and beat it in lightly with the balloon whisk.

2. Add the oil a few drops at a time beating all the time with the balloon whisk. It will eventually become thick and pale after which you can add the oil a little more quickly. If it becomes

TIPS & TECHNIQUES

When making mayonnaise it is important that the oil does not curdle the eggs, which is why it must be added very carefully to start with.

The initial addition of the salt helps the egg to cream with the oil. Once it is obviously thick and pale one can proceed more quickly.

Do not add the other ingredients until you know it has started to thicken properly.

For a healthier option use olive oil or a mixture of oils. Experiment to find what suits you best. Similarly with the vinegar and lemon juice. The juice can be a bit sharp.

The more egg white you leave with the yolks the lighter will be your final product. If making a double quantity, an easy proportion is 3 egg yolks + 1 whole egg.

A garlic crusher is really needed for the Aioli recipe, but if you have to crush the garlic by hand first crush it with the flat blade of a knife; put some salt on it then chop finely.

Aioli or Ali-oli was being made at least as early as Roman days. It is said that the French when they discovered it in Mahon in the Balearic

too thick add a little of the vinegar or lemon juice.

3. Add the rest of the ingredients and continue with the balloon whisk, adding more vinegar or lemon juice to taste.

Pickled Eggs ☐

Utensils
A large saucepan for the eggs
A saucepan for the vinegar
A bowl of cold water
Large glass jar or jars with open necks and screw tops

Ingredients
Enough eggs to fill your jar(s)
Enough vinegar to cover the eggs in the jars
A tbsp pickling spices

Method

1. Heat the water in the saucepan and before it boils, add the eggs carefully so they do not crack. Bring to the boil and simmer for 5 minutes.

2. Remove the eggs to the bowl of cold water and shell them when they are cool enough to handle.

3. Meanwhile, bring the vinegar with the spices to the boil. Remove from the

Islands, took it home, removed the garlic and called it Mahon-aise. In those days garlic was used in peasant cooking to perk up the flavours, and it was considered to have no place in 'haute cuisine'. Fashions changed and the French eventually liked to add the garlic back in again.

If you prefer a simple mayonnaise, just leave out the garlic and reduce the quantity of mustard.

Pickled eggs *may be kept a long time, so you need to use good-quality eggs, but they should not be so fresh that you cannot peel them. (See T & T page 15).*

Whole Pickling Spices *can be purchased from any good supermarket. They are a mixture of different coloured peppercorns, cloves, dried chili, etc.*

Distilled malt vinegar *is best for pickled eggs as it leaves the eggs looking nice and white, but it is not always obtainable. White wine vinegar is a good substitute and even plain malt vinegar can be used, though it discolours the eggs.*

Pickled eggs will keep for more than a year, and in fact are not ready for eating until 2 or 3 weeks after pickling.

They are ideal for adding to a

heat and allow to cool.

4. Put a little cold vinegar in the jar, add the eggs, topping up with vinegar until it is full, making sure that all are completely covered.

Orange Marmalade with Coriander ☐

Utensils
A good chopping board and sharp knife
A large saucepan
Some muslin or material from a pair of tights *(and don't ask why Baggy would have a pair of tights lying around!)*
Jam jars preferably with screw tops

Ingredients
6 oranges or 4 oranges & 2 lemons
1 tbs coriander seeds
2 lbs (1 kilo) sugar
4 cups of water

Method

1. Cut the oranges into quarters on your chopping board and squeeze the juice from each quarter into your saucepan, removing the pips as you go. Now slice each quarter with your sharp knife as finely as you want.

2. Put the coriander seeds into the material and crush them through the

salad or simply cutting into sections and serving as an aperitif perhaps mixed with some pieces of cucumber or celery.

Making marmalade *in the days of Baggy's childhood meant that a whole day was set aside for it. Nothing else could disturb his mother while she sliced and cooked in a huge preserving pan enough oranges to make marmalade to last through the year, plus enough to give away as presents to neighbours (usually in exchange for one made to the neighbour's recipe).*

It could only be done when Seville oranges arrived in the shops for it was the only time when oranges were cheap enough to use in this way, and accounted for the bitter flavour of the product, for Seville oranges were only cheap because they were no use for anything else.

Sweet oranges can be equally well used, and in fact make a more pleasant, sweeter product with less added sugar.

It is not necessary to make large quantities of marmalade or jam. If space is limited make half the quantity given opposite.

Coriander seeds *when crushed exude a wonderful orangey scent and make an excellent addition*

fabric with the back of a wooden spoon or rolling pin. Tie them up in the fabric with a bit of cotton. Add the bag to the oranges.

3. Add the water and leave overnight. This will soften the peel and swell it, so bear this in mind when you are cutting the peel and keep it fine.

4. Bring the oranges to the boil and simmer uncovered, stirring occasionally until the peel is soft.

5. Add the sugar, stirring all the time until it is melted, then bring the marmalade to the boil and keep it bubbling well until you eventually see the bubbles getting smaller and the whole thing thickening up a bit. It should start to thicken on the side of the pan too.

6. Let it rest off the boil then pour or ladle it into the jars. Seal them while it is still hot.

Blackberry & Elderberry Jelly □ *

Utensils
A large, wide saucepan
A second wide bowl or pan
A pint measure, or measuring jug
A square of muslin or loose-weaved material.

to marmalade giving it a spicy tang.

Once the sugar is added the fruit will not soften any more – in fact it may harden up slightly. So cook the fruit until it is soft enough before adding the sugar. This applies to any jam or marmalade.

A pressure cooker *can be used to cook the fruit before adding the sugar. This saves time and energy.*

The most difficult thing *about making marmalade or jams is to know when it is ready for putting in the jars. Baggy did not know about jam-thermometers and such like, but he learnt eventually to know when it was ready from how the mixture looked. He noticed the bubbles became smaller and closer together as the liquid thickened.*

He remembered his mother putting a little bit on a saucer and placing it in the fridge then when the sample set with a skin on the top she knew it was ready. But for these small amounts it took too long for the sample to set at all and Baggy usually ended up licking the warm sticky mixture off the saucer.

To tell if you have a successful set *in your jars, allow it to cool, put one jar in the fridge to really cool down, then pick it up, hold your breath, and tip it sideways. For a*

A length of string formed into a loop
A place to hang the bag of fruit
Jam jars with lids

Ingredients
A mixture of fresh-picked blackberries and elderberries, in any proportion
12 oz (335 g) sugar to each pint of juice produced
Juice of 1 lemon

Method

1. Wash the fruit and remove any unwanted bits and stalks. No need to be too fussy as you will only be using the juice.

2. Place the fruit in a large pan with a very little water and cook gently until the fruit is cooked, stirring occasionally to make sure it does not burn on the bottom. Mash it with a potato masher or squash the fruit as much as possible to let out the juice.

3. Drape the muslin over the second bowl or pan and tip the mixture into it. Pull the sides of the muslin up and put the loop of string round the top and through itself again so that it tightens as you lift it.

4. Hang the other end of the noose over a convenient cupboard door knob, hook, or handle, and let the liquid drip into the receptacle underneath. Leave

good strong marmalade you should be able to tip it upside down.

If it is very runny there is no alternative but to put it all back in the saucepan and boil it up again. Cook it once more until you know it will be OK.

Sealing the jars *when they are still hot creates a slight vacuum inside which prevents mould from forming. Well-made and well-sealed preserves with metal screw tops will keep for 3 years without spoiling, so long as you don't break the vacuum by unscrewing the top to see how it is getting on!*

Coffee jars *with plastic lids are not suitable for preserving as the plastic does not seal well enough to form a vacuum. They can be used if you are going to eat the produce fairly quickly.*

Jam from any fruit *can be made by following the basic marmalade recipe with the addition of lemon juice in the proportion of approx. ½ a lemon to 1 lb of fruit. 12 oz – 1 lb sugar should be added to each 1 lb of fruit depending on the sweetness of the fruit.*

Making jelly *can be very rewarding and makes a lovely present when it is clear and so colourful.*

for at least 12 hours.

5. When convenient, measure the liquid and add the sugar in the proportion of ¾ lb to one pint of liquid. Add the lemon juice. Bring to the boil, and proceed as for marmalade.

Pesto ✓ ☐

Utensils
A pestle and mortar or an electric blender

Ingredients
1 clove garlic, finely chopped or crushed
1 handful of fresh basil leaves, chopped
1 tbsp pine nuts
1 tbsp parmesan cheese, grated
5 fl oz (150 ml) olive oil (approx)
Salt & pepper

Method

1. Put all the dry ingredients + half the olive oil into a pestle and mortar or blender and thoroughly combine them. Add more olive oil until it is a good firm consistency. Put it in a jar and keep in the fridge until needed.

The instructions for jelly may look complicated but it falls into two separate operations: 1) cooking the fruit and hanging the bag. The resulting juice will happily sit in the fridge if necessary until you are ready for part 2) boiling the juice with the sugar and putting it in the jars.

Blackberries and elderberries produce their fruit at the same time of year and grow in the same place, so are easy to pick together.

The basic jelly recipe *can be used with any fruit with pips that you want to remove e.g. raspberries, loganberries or redcurrants.*

Lemon juice *is an essential ingredient as it contains the pectin that makes the jelly or jam set.*

Any open-weave material can be used for the jelly bag but check first that it is porous enough for liquid to pass through. Make sure it is large enough; there is nothing more annoying than finding the fruit spilling over.

Pesto *is a useful addition to spaghetti or other pasta for a quick tasty meal.*

Basil *or Vasillica is a lovely herb with a delicate scent and an individual flavour. Distinctly Mediterranean, the scent reminds one*

Pickled Capers ✓ ☐ *

Utensils
1 bowl
Small jars

Ingredients
Buds from the caper plant
Vinegar, preferably white wine or cider vinegar
Water
1 tbsp salt

Method

1. Soak the caper buds in water for three days, changing the water daily.

2. Mix enough water and vinegar in equal quantities to cover the caper buds; add the salt.

3. Drain the capers; pack them in the jars and cover with the liquid mixture. Keep for 2 – 3 weeks before using.

Ginger Beer ☐ *

Utensils
Bowl, pan or bucket large enough to hold 1 gallon or 5 litres of boiling water
Sieve or colander
Funnel or jug for pouring
5 x 1 litre plastic bottles, or equivalent

of wild Greek hillsides.

As parsley is to an English housewife, so Basil is to anyone living on the shores of the Mediterranean. You will find it growing in tin cans on the doorstep of the poorest household.

In Turkey the traditional boats stand a large pot of the small-leafed variety at the top of the companionway and anyone who passes trails their fingers through it so that the scent sweetens the air and helps to keep flies away.

The caper bush *is a very pretty plant that grows in profusion in dry Mediterranean countries. It will sprout from any crack in concrete or stone, or weave its way through stony hedgerows.*

Every part of the plant is said to be edible and many parts are medicinal; the buds are said to be good for rheumatism. The flowers are exquisite. Such a wonderful plant must have a downside and the caper has the most vicious curved thorns to protect its fruit and flowers – so beware!

Only the unopened buds should be used and the best way to pick the buds (early in the morning before the heat gets on them) is to delicately nip the stem behind the bud

Ingredients

½ a fresh root ginger; or 1 oz (28 g) dried root ginger soaked in water.
2 lemons
1 lb (450 g) sugar
1 gallon (5 litres) water, some of which needs to be boiling
½ pkt. dried yeast

Method

1. Chop the root ginger and place it in the bucket together with the sugar.

2. Wash the lemons and remove the peel without cutting into the white pith. Place the peel in the bowl. Remove the pith and discard. Now slice the lemons across the segments and add the slices to the bowl. Add the sugar.

3. Meanwhile bring the water to the boil and pour it over the mixture. Stir until the sugar is dissolved then allow it to stand covered with a tea towel until it is warm to the touch but neither hot nor cold. At this point sprinkle the yeast over the top and after ½ hour give it a good stir.

4. Leave the mixture for 2 - 3 days, stirring twice a day.

5. Strain the liquid into the bottles and put on the tops. Keep for another 2 - 3 days before opening. If the bottles swell with finger and thumbnail.

Pickled capers can be added to mayonnaise or aioli to make a very tasty Tartare Sauce. They can be mixed in any salad, and are useful in many fish dishes.

The Ginger Beer recipe is a typical old fashioned one that would have been made during the summer in any country household before the days of mass-marketing.

Beware! Baggy's version is relatively alcoholic because the longer you keep it the more the yeast eats up the sugar, so it also becomes less sweet. Baggy himself sometimes wondered at first why this innocuous, refreshing lunchtime drink had him falling asleep in the afternoon. Some of Baggy's unsuspecting guests would stagger home after thinking they had imbibed a pleasant soft drink rather than a lunchtime beer!

The remaining fruit is what is known as 'a ginger beer plant'. This is because you can use it again and again as it just keeps on growing. It will keep covered in the fridge until required.

When making the next batch it is a good idea to add half the quantity of each of the ingredients and throw away any bits of lemon that have gone soggy.

alarmingly (which they may do the first night) loosen the cap to let some gas out.

Hot Sweet Chutney ✓ ☐

Utensils
Saucepan
Jars with lids

Ingredients
1 lb (500 g) dried apricots
1 lb (500 g) dates or raisins, stoned
½ lb (250 g) preserved ginger OR
1 tbsp ground ginger
2 large onions
2 cloves garlic
3 red chillies
1 lb (500 g) sugar
1 tsp salt
¾ pt (370 ml) vinegar

Method

1. Soak apricots overnight.

2. Chop finely the fruit, onions, garlic, chillies, and preserved ginger.

3. Bring all the ingredients to the boil together; simmer for ½ hour then allow to get cool before putting into jars. Seal well.

Chutney *is a very useful item to have in the store cupboard, either as a handy present to give to someone, or to bring out when a meal looks a bit plain.*

Chutney goes well with cold meats and cheese.

A spoonful will perk up a dish like the Savoury Bread and Butter Pudding, mixed in on one of the layers or served in a separate dish.

These sort of preserves need to be kept for a while before the flavours meld and blend.

The longer you keep them the better they will become, so be sure that you have sealed the jars well.

Always mark your jars with the ingredients and the date. Even if you think you will remember what it is, it is still nice to be reminded where and when you found the ingredients. It is also good if giving it as a present.

CHAPTER 11: ALBERTINA

Baggy enjoyed sailing to Tunisia with its hospitable people, the total change of culture, the completely different landscapes and harbours. But the weather was not just getting hot; it was getting unbearable - as were the flies and the unsubtle smells. So he set sail again on *The Sea Crow* and headed away from the sandy, prawn-breeding shores of the African coast towards more sophisticated ports. Once again he moored his yacht stern-to the quay in a lively tourist resort where he could sit in his cockpit and watch the holidaymakers parading along the seafront.

The Captain of *The Sea Crow* was by this time not quite the same person who had left Brighton marina with his wife and dreams. Nor was he quite the same man who had sailed away from the Balearics alone. He was now a leaner and fitter man, tanned to a chestnut brown (almost) all over, and the crinkles beside his eyes enhanced their compelling blue. Moreover, he handled his rather large yacht with a nonchalant aplomb, which caused locals to address him as Captain, Capitano, or Capitan depending on the language of the country. He had learnt never to run on his boat, never to shout in anger or in trepidation; never to throw a line until he knew it would reach. The seafaring wisdom of Old Captain Baggywrinkle was in his veins and it had only needed a bit of seasoning to bring it out in his son.

In return for the compliment of being addressed as Captain, he would call "Captain, Sir!" to any jumped-up harbour official in a fancy cap and thus ensured an easy passage through the tide-rips of foreign officialdom. To pink-cheeked, nervous skippers mooring their chartered yacht for the first time, he would call "Well done, Captain!" to the delight of the recipient and his over-awed family, encouraging a friendly atmosphere along the quayside.

So it was not surprising that a number of tourists passing by, stopped to talk to Captain B. and quite a few of them were decidedly attractive young ladies. One Italian lady in particular returned several times until Captain B. invited her on board for a glass of wine. He soon suggested dinner though in such a way that it was not quite clear whether he meant dinner on shore 'au restaurant' or dinner on board, which would have suited Baggy's pocket better.

Albertina was no spring chicken but nor was Captain B and she had sized him up as being just about what she needed. She had quickly ascertained that he was alone – and had been for quite some time. She was also keen to see the inside of the yacht so she offered to bring dinner with her when she returned in one hour. Baggy was over the moon. He laid the table, brought out a candle, and played a CD of his most romantic music. Then he sat wondering what she would bring for dinner and just – <u>how</u>? And while he waited he started to wonder what he might cook for Albertina on another occasion. By this time he had devised his very own Moussagna – an amalgam of an Italian lasagne and a Greek moussaka.

When Albertina returned it was not with a steaming tureen of seafood pasta, but with care she carried a packet of spaghetti, a tin of tomatoes and "ze zecret ingredient" which turned out to be a stock cube. Another small packet contained two pieces of shop-cooked chicken.

"I can zee you do not eat properly," she exclaimed, giving him a sly pinch in the ribs. "I a-cook for you a big spaghetti." And with that she set to and in no time at all produced an excellent dish, while Baggy wondered if he had become too complicated about his cooking.

It was not quite the romantic dinner he would have planned himself, as they tore the chicken flesh from the bones and slurped at the spaghetti, but their eyes spoke what their mouths could not and it was quite soon after the meal that they rolled into the luxurious bed in the aft-cabin.

RECIPES

Albertina's Spaghetti ✓ ☐

Utensils
1 small saucepan
1 large saucepan

Ingredients
5 oz (140g) spaghetti
¼ onion, finely chopped
1 tin tomatoes
1 chicken or vegetable stock cube
2 tbsp olive oil
½ tsp basil (dried) or 2 sprigs of fresh chopped basil
Salt & pepper
Parmesan cheese for topping

Method

1. In a small saucepan, heat the olive oil and cook the onion until it just begins to turn brown.

2. Meanwhile put a large pan of salted water on to boil with a little oil in it.

3. Add the tomatoes to the onion, breaking up any whole ones. Crumble in the dry stock cube.

4. Add the basil, salt & pepper. Stir well.

TIPS & TECHNIQUES

Fresh Pasta is far superior to packet pasta, but the recipes here assume the use of the packet variety for convenience sake.

If you have the opportunity to buy fresh pasta make the most of it, but no recipes are given here as it is such an individual product varying according to the maker.

Timing *is one of the most important aspects of cooking, if you want all parts of the meal to be ready at the same time. Once you have mastered this concept, everything else will fall into place.*

When entertaining in particular it is easier to think backwards so that you get an order in your mind of what needs doing first and what needs to be left to the last minute so that everything is ready for the table at the same time.

The meal opposite, for example, takes 30 minutes for the sauce, 10 minutes for the spaghetti and perhaps 3 minutes for some frozen peas to accompany it.

Start with the sauce and once it is under way put on the water for the spaghetti. 15 minutes before you

5. Leave it to cook on a moderate heat so that the liquid reduces and thickens.

6. When the water boils in the large saucepan, add the spaghetti, stir it and cook for 10 – 15 minutes.

7. Strain the spaghetti, return it to the saucepan and 'air' it (see T & T page 103).

Serve with the sauce and a topping of Parmesan cheese.

Spaghetti alla Carbonara ✓

Utensils
1 large saucepan
1 frying pan
Bowl for the eggs

Ingredients
5 oz (140g) spaghetti
2 slices of bacon, chopped
1 clove of garlic, crushed
2 eggs
A spoonful of crème fraise or a dash of thick cream
Salt & pepper
A dash of paprika or Tabasco
A knob of butter
Parmesan cheese for topping

want to eat put the spaghetti in the water. Ten minutes later put a little water on to boil for the peas. Since the peas will only need to cook for 3 minutes, all should be ready at the same time.

Be sure to have your sauce as-near-as-damn-it ready before you let the spaghetti anywhere near the boiling water. You don't want to be trying to hurry the sauce while the spaghetti is going soggy. It sounds obvious but many people learn it the hard way.

*'**Al Dente**' as the Italians say, or 'with a bite to it,' is how spaghetti or any kind of pasta should be served. Don't overcook it and never leave it in the water after it is ready as it will continue to cook and lose its 'bite'.*

***To help prevent spaghetti or pasta sticking** in the pan, add a few drops of oil to the water.*

If you do end up with a stodgy mass this must be due to: lack of sufficient water in the pan, overcooking, and/or inferior grade of pasta.

The antidote is to drain it and pour fresh boiling water over it.

It is always best to buy good quality products. It is worth the extra money and will make the difference

Method

1. In a large saucepan bring plenty of salted water to the boil and cook the spaghetti until 'al dente' (10 - 15 minutes).

2. Meanwhile fry the bacon in a little butter, adding the chopped garlic halfway through.

3. Beat the eggs in the bowl with the crème fraise or cream, salt, pepper and paprika.

4. Drain the spaghetti; return it to the pan and pour in the egg mixture off the heat. The spaghetti should be hot enough to cook the eggs in its own heat as you mix it in.

5. Add the bacon with any residue from the pan and serve sprinkled with Parmesan cheese.

Moussagna □ *
(For 4 people)

Utensils
Large deep frying pan
Large saucepan
Casserole dish
Gas ring
Oven preheated to gas mk. 5

between nice clean looking pasta and soft starchy pasta.

All the above tips also apply to rice.

It will make all the difference to your spaghetti if you 'air' it after you have drained off the water. To do this, take two forks and lift the strands of spaghetti to separate and aerate it.

If you wish you can at that time add any or all of the following: a knob of butter, freshly ground black pepper, parsley, or a little bit of the sauce you intend to eat with it.

If you have pasta left over, you can re-heat it later by simply throwing it into boiling salted water for 2 minutes.

***The Moussagna** was Baggy's special entertainment dish and evolved out of different attempts at making Greek Moussaka and Italian Lasagne.*

Although it is more complicated than anything so far, it has the advantage of being able to be made in different phases and will happily sit around until ready to be cooked, re-cooked, or finally put together.

Ingredients

A quantity of Bolognaise Sauce (page 73)
1 aubergine
Olive oil
8 slices lasagne (preferably green)
1 quantity white sauce (see below)
Soft white breadcrumbs (optional)
1 - 2 oz (40 g) cooking cheese

Ingredients for the white sauce:
2 oz (56 g) butter or margarine
2 heaped tbsp plain flour
1 pt (450 ml) milk
Salt & pepper
A pinch of nutmeg
1 beaten egg (optional)

Method

PHASE 1: AUBERGINES
Prepare the aubergine by slicing lengthwise into pieces ½" (1 cm) thick, sprinkle with salt and leave for ½ to 1 hour to drain. Shake the moisture off and pat dry with kitchen paper.

In a large deep frying pan heat the oil and fry the slices of aubergine until brown on each side. Place the slices side by side to cover the bottom of the casserole dish and sprinkle them with the white breadcrumbs.

PHASE 2: BOLOGNESE SAUCE
Make a quantity of Baggy's Bolognaise Sauce in the same frying pan (no need

Aubergines *are an exotic-looking vegetable with a deep purple skin and pleasing shape. One can't resist buying them in the market but then what do you do with them? They become a shiny, inedible ornament that slowly deteriorates while you promise yourself to cook it tomorrow.*

The Turks have invented hundreds of recipes for them, mostly involving the work of a little old grandmother with nothing else to do. But they are a 'meaty' vegetable and make a small amount of meat go a long way.

Green Pasta *is often found in the shops and has slightly more flavour and substance to it. It also makes a pasta dish look more interesting. The colour is imparted by the addition of spinach.*

White Sauce *is the basis of many every-day and classic dishes so it is worth persevering with so that you can make it quickly and easily when required. It is a basic recipe that leads to Béchamel Sauce, Cheese Sauce, Parsley Sauce and many others.*

Even if you have to measure the ingredients the first time you make it, try to be brave enough to do it without having to measure.

You can measure the amount

to wash it first).

PHASE 3: LASAGNE

Cook the lasagne in a large pan of boiling water for 10 mins. Drain and cover with cold water until needed, checking that the leaves are not sticking together.

PHASE 4: MAKE THE WHITE SAUCE:

1. Melt the butter in a pan on a low heat and add enough flour to absorb the butter, stirring well.

2. Add the milk a dash at a time, stirring to make a paste, gradually thinning to a thick sauce.

3. Add salt, pepper, nutmeg or mace to the white sauce as you go.

4. You now have a basic white sauce, but for a true moussaka (or moussagna) remove it from the heat and stir in the beaten egg.

PHASE 5 PUTTING IT TOGETHER

1. Spoon a little Bolognese Sauce over the aubergines in the bottom of the casserole dish. Cover with a layer of lasagne.

2. Add another layer of Bolognaise sauce then a little of the white sauce (about 1/3 of the total quantity), then another layer of lasagne. (These layers can be increased or diminished

of butter you need by judging it as a proportion of the whole pack.

Gently add enough flour to absorb the amount of fat you started with.

Add the milk gently until the sauce is the consistency you require.

Keep the heat low unless you get bored and want to hurry things up.

Make sure you stir into the corners or edges of the saucepan, and across the middle, rather than just round and round in the same place.

If the butter or margarine goes brown before you have started adding the flour, you may as well just throw it away and start again with fresh ingredients!

Margarine will burn more easily than butter. A little olive oil added to butter helps to prevent it burning.

The Moussagna can be left to rest for up to 12 hours if required.

To re-heat it, it can be placed in a microwave to save time before putting it in the oven.

If the dish seems rather full, place a baking tray underneath it in the oven to catch any drips.

according to the size of your dish).

3. Place all the leftover sauce on top of the lasagne then sprinkle the cheese over the top.

4. Cook in a medium oven until the top is brown.

Liver in Orange Sauce ✓ *

<u>Utensils</u>
Frying pan
1 gas ring

<u>Ingredients</u>
8 oz (225 g) lamb or calves liver thinly sliced
1 oz. flour
½ tsp. dried thyme (or mixed herbs)
Oil, salt & pepper
Juice of 1 orange
A little grated orange rind (optional)

<u>Method</u>

1. Mix the thyme, salt and pepper and the grated orange if using it with the flour. Coat the slices of liver in the mixture.

2. Fry the liver slices quickly in the oil on either side. Add the orange juice and simmer for 3 – 5 minutes.

Liver is one of those dishes that some people hate and others love, but with the addition of the orange everybody seems to like it.

This easy liver dish is very nice served with rice or pasta.

Lambs liver is the best, then calves liver. Ox liver can be tough. Avoid pigs liver which has a strong flavour.

Always remove any pieces of gristle or tubes from the liver before cooking.

Thyme *is one of the main ingredients of Mixed Herbs. It has a lovely scent and dries well. It makes a nice bush, easily grown in a pot. It can also be found growing wild.*

When using any fresh herbs you need double the quantity given for dried herbs.

Fresh thyme is much better for the liver dish. Remove any stalks.

CHAPTER 12 : THE RAT RACE

With his large, rather smart yacht and his increasing culinary skills combined with his equally decreasing income as interest rates on his capital fell, it did occur to Baggy that he could earn a bob or two by taking paying guests on board. So he was quite pleased when a business friend from his working days called him to say that he would like to come and stay for a week with his new lady-friend – a kind of pre-nuptial honeymoon. He remembered his old friend as a rather high-flying businessman who would expect the best and even so Baggy was happy to give it a go.

This is why he was thrashing to windward to get to his pick-up point with a tasty casserole in his slow-cooker. Not long before he reached his destination he realised oil was leaking from some unseen part of his engine. Sod's law! Never mind, he had allowed himself plenty of time and would drop anchor as close as possible to a boatyard he knew well and get it mended. It was a dingy part of town but he got the work done – just a new gasket and a mucky job to fit it. Tired from his day's work he spent the night at anchor off the boatyard.

He had moved out of his luxurious aft-cabin so that it was ready for the arrival of the pre-honeymooners in a couple of days, whilst he slept in the lower berth of the middle cabin. That night he was woken by something fast and furry running across his bunk and into the saloon. Was he dreaming? As he walked into the saloon he just caught sight of the furry creature running back over his bunk and out of the open hatch. Several large bites had been taken out of the ripe peaches in his fruit bowl. A rat! Somehow a rat must have come on board from the boatyard. This was the last thing he needed with his honeymooners soon to arrive. In this hot weather they would be sure to want the hatch over the top of the big double bed open, and if the furry creature rushed in over their bed the way it had run over his own bunk – well, it did not bear thinking about!

Early morning saw him at the shops buying an assortment of rat traps, which he primed with tasty cheese and spread around the saloon with the fruit bowl removed. Sure enough, with the hatch open through the hot night, the furry creature with the long tail scurried in. Baggy stayed in bed with his ears straining to hear the sound of a trap snapping shut. He heard scuffling and scrapings but then the creature scurried out again over his bed and onto the deck. Unbelievable! All the traps with their tasty cheese morsels were untouched, but a bag of tomatoes in the galley had been attacked and a bite taken out of each one!

With his guests arriving that evening he had to find where the rat was hiding. He searched everywhere and the only possible place was the anchor locker – the place it must have first discovered as it climbed up the anchor chain. Baggy set the biggest trap – a cage that would catch the rat alive – and laid it carefully in the anchor locker, baited with pieces of peach and tomato, for this rat was thirsty rather than hungry and had already ignored his tasty cheese.

Baggy was genuinely pleased to see his old friend with his smart new lady-friend but as he poured the welcoming glasses of champagne there was a lead weight near to panic in his stomach. It was a magic evening as they set off into the sunset, and as the sun reached the horizon the yacht turned into the bay in which they would spend the night at anchor. It could not have been more peaceful.

Baggy left the two love-birds in the cockpit while he went forward to get the anchor ready for dropping. He opened the hatch and there inside the cage was the rat staring up at him with bright beady eyes. Never had Baggy been more pleased to see a rat! With his body shielding the sight from his guests, he picked the cage up, rat and all, and dropped it quickly over the side of the boat.

"Swimming lessons for you!" he muttered, as he wiped the sweat from his brow and heaved a sigh of relief.

RECIPES

Fish Pâté ✓ ☐ *

Utensils
Mixing bowl or liquidiser
Ramekin dishes or small bowls

Ingredients
4 oz (110 g) cold, leftover fish such as mackerel, herring, salmon, tuna etc
1 cup of soft white breadcrumbs
1 tbsp Baggy's Garlic Mayonnaise (page 90) or 1 tbsp mayonnaise and ½ clove garlic, crushed
½ tsp paprika, or Tabasco Sauce
Salt & pepper

Method

1. Mix all the ingredients together and mash them well in a bowl or mix in a liquidiser.

2. Taste, and adjust the seasoning. If necessary add a little more mayonnaise to get a good consistency where it all holds together.

3. Transfer to small ramekin dishes or bowls and store in the fridge or freezer.

This will keep for a surprisingly long time as the paprika, garlic and mayonnaise all help to preserve the fish.

TIPS & TECHNIQUES

The recipes in this section are suitable for smarter dining, though the methods are really just as simple as anything else.

Chili powder, cayenne pepper or Tabasco Sauce is an essential ingredient for the Fish Pâté. It prevents it from being too bland and helps to preserve the fish.

The fish pâté is just one of the dishes that are made simply by the inclusion of the homemade garlic mayonnaise described on page 90.

It makes a good, easy starter at a dinner party in ramekin dishes, served with a little garnish and some toast.

***Prawns** can mean different things to different people. If you are accustomed to catching your own when the tide turns on a sandy English beach, with your trousers rolled up and toes going numb, you will probably be thinking of what is technically called a shrimp.*

If you come from South Africa or Florida a mere prawn is probably what you or I would call a Langoustine.

Somewhere in between is a

Prawns in Garlic & Cream Sauce ✓∗

Utensils
Frying pan

Ingredients
½ lb (250 g) (A good handful) per person of uncooked prawns in their shells
1 oz (28 g) butter (size of ½ egg)
1 clove garlic
1 tbsp fresh parsley (chopped)
Salt & pepper (preferably fresh ground mixed pepper)
1 tbsp dry sherry or white wine
1 tbsp cream, or crème fraise
Wedge of lemon for garnish

Method

1. Wash the prawns well in fresh, salted water.

2. In the frying pan melt the butter. Squeeze the clove of garlic into it and throw in the prawns. Sprinkle with a little salt and plenty of pepper.

3. Move the prawns and turn them in the butter for a couple of minutes, until they have changed colour. They are done as soon as they are opaque - don't over-do them.

4. Add a splash of dry sherry and raise the heat very briefly.

juicy, tender, thin-shelled delicacy 3 or 4 inches long.

For the recipe opposite, any will do as long as they are large enough to be eaten by hand.

For average to large prawns the black vein down the back should be removed. This is a tedious but not too difficult a job. Shell the prawns and slice down the back with a sharp pointed knife. The black vein, which is the gut of the animal, can be easily seen and pulled out.

With shelled prawns *you can use the same recipe opposite but add some baby artichoke hearts and some pink gilled mushrooms at the same time as you cook the prawns. This makes a more formal meal, and a delicious one.*

Dried Parsley *has a faint smell of hay and no taste at all. So if you want the real taste of parsley it must be fresh.*

Luckily it is usually readily available - either the curly bright green English variety or the flat leafed variety more common in warmer countries.

You can keep a few sprigs fresh for a while in a jar of water in the kitchen, or in a plastic bag in the fridge. It will also freeze.

5. Remove from the heat and stir ½ the parsley and all the cream gently into the dish. Sprinkle the rest of the parsley over the top and garnish with the lemon.

Unbelievably delicious! If making this just for yourself you can eat them straight from the pan with a chunk of fresh bread to mop up the juices. Mmmm!

Gougière *

Utensils
Saucepan
Baking tray or ring mould
Measuring jug
Oven preheated to gas mk. 7

Ingredients
Basic choux pastry:
2 ½ oz (70 g) plain flour
2 oz butter
2 eggs, beaten
5 fl oz (110 ml) cold water

For Gougière:
2 ½ oz grated cheese
½ tsp mustard
Cayenne pepper or Tabasco Sauce
Salt & freshly ground pepper

Parsley is very good for you. It contains lots of vitamin C and helps to purify the blood.

Before indulging *in the prawns, have ready beside your plate a bowl of water with a slice of lemon in it, along with a good paper napkin.*

Remember - the lemon will take the smell from your fingers – and from the frying pan afterward.

Mixed ground pepper *is wonderful for seafood dishes. More aromatic than black pepper, the subtle, delicate flavour blends perfectly with shellfish.*

Crème Fraise *is not fresh cream as the name implies, but it is a very useful substitute. It is sour cream with some useful additions that make it glutinous and easy to spoon from the tub.*

It is a bit more user-friendly than real cream and will not curdle so easily if inadvertently brought to the boil.

Neither cream nor crème fraise should ever be boiled, but just gently heated with the food at the end of the cooking.

Gougière *is a traditional French recipe which is surprisingly*

Method

1. Put the water, butter, salt & pepper in the saucepan and bring it just to the boil. Remove from heat.

2. Shoot the flour into the pan all at once and beat it round and round so that there are no lumps. It will make quite a stiff mixture.

3. Now add the beaten eggs a bit at a time, still beating until they are all absorbed.

4. Finally add the grated cheese, mustard and Tabasco Sauce or cayenne pepper. Beat it well again.

5. Spoon it in little dollops onto the baking tray, or preferably into the ring mould but still in individual mounds.

6. Bake in the pre-heated oven at gas mk. 7 for 20 - 25 minutes.

Pastry Puffs *
(Makes 6)

Utensils
Floured baking tray

Ingredients
12 oz (336 g) pkt Frozen Puff Pastry (defrosted)

easy to make yet is rarely seen. It makes a lovely supplement to a salad lunch especially when cooked in the ring mould and served as a round with slices of Parma ham crinkled up between each mound, and some green salad in the centre.

*A **ring mould** is the same shape as a jelly mould with a hole in the middle, but it is used for baking. It saves cooking time and is useful for the Gougière where a high heat is needed all around the ingredients.*

If using the little rounds on the baking tray, they can be filled with a herby cream cheese.

***Choux Pastry** in the form of little buns is the recipe for that favourite dessert Profiteroles. Just add a little sugar instead of the seasoning. The buns are finally filled with cream and topped with a chocolate sauce or melted cooking chocolate.*

***Puff pastry** is not easy to make successfully and the frozen packets are so good there seems little point in going to the extra trouble of making it.*

These Pastry Puffs can equally well be made with pieces of fish, or a mixture of fish and shellfish.

The recipe is very economical on the meat – be careful your pieces

10 oz (280 g) chicken breast divided into 6 pieces and seasoned with grated lemon rind, salt & pepper

A small quantity of thick white/parsley sauce (see page 68 & 104) with a dash of dry sherry added, used cold.

A little extra milk

Method

1. Divide the puff pastry into 6 portions and roll each one out.

2. Place a piece of chicken on each piece of pastry, adding a dollop of the cold parsley sauce.

3. Fold up the edges to make a parcel, sealing them together with water or milk. Brush more milk over the top.

4. Place on a baking tray sprinkled with flour and bake in the oven for 20 - 30 minutes.

are not too big for the pastry to wrap around.

Make sure the white/parsley sauce is thick enough and cold, otherwise it will run away before you make it into a parcel.

Individual Beef Wellingtons can be made in the same way with a portion of fillet beef and Duxelles Sauce (see page 47) for the filling.

If you want to be special save a little extra pastry and put the initial of each guest in pastry on top of each individual puff.

Any pieces of extra pastry from whatever recipe, can be made into anchovy sticks or cheese sticks to go with an aperitif. (See T & T page 55)

Garlic Mayonnaise makes a perfect dip for the pastry sticks, especially with a little blue cheese and/or Tabasco sauce added.

CHAPTER 13:   TURKISH MARKET

When Bill Baggy reached Turkey he simply relaxed, as he had never done since he was a child. He had crossed the Mediterranean almost from end to end and there was no longer any pressure to move on or to achieve a new goal. Somehow, the tiredness of decades of hard work crept up on him and he whiled away his days in a lazy haze. *The Sea Crow* rested too, rocking gently to her anchor in idyllic bays of clear blue water fringed with pine trees rustling in the breeze. Although he was alone he did not feel lonely but revelled in his self-sufficiency and his harmony with the natural elements.

In fact there was plenty of company from the owners of other yachts whom he had met along the way and frequent invitations for 'a sundowner' and offers to swap some of the few English books in circulation. If he had a problem on the boat he could not solve, a spare part he could not find, trouble he could not locate – there was always someone to ask who had been there before him.

The stream of charter yachts that came and went provided him with continual entertainment. He admired the way the Turkish skippers moored their huge *gulets* - dropping their anchors on the approach, twisting, and mooring with long lines tied to the rocks - and he chuckled sympathetically over the antics of holiday-charterers attempting the same manoeuvre for the first time.

It was easy to understand why the Turkish cuisine centred around vegetable dishes. Here the vegetables were grown in real earth, ripened under the warm sun and picked at dawn with the dew still glistening on them. Shopping on market day was an event in itself. Early in the morning Baggy would go ashore in his dinghy with his straw hat on his head and straw basket in hand. Many of the stallholders would have come in from the surrounding country villages with whatever was in season on their land. The country-folk sat with their bowls of homemade yoghurt, the best honey from their bees, a few eggs from their hens and whatever fruit or vegetables were in season. The professionals offered new leather bags and belts, shiny pots and pans, brightly coloured kiddies' toys. Some of the stallholders knew him by sight now and welcomed him as a friend. They all liked to practise their tourist-English while he tried out the few Turkish words he had learnt and practiced his bartering skills.

By mid-day he would be loaded down with his purchases. A cold beer was necessary so he would join a variety of friends at a dusty street-side sandwich bar where they would joke and gossip an hour away. Then with the afternoon breeze perhaps causing a little anxiety over the firmness of their anchors, the members of the little group would drift off and jostle their way through the market-day crowds, back to their dinghies and thence to their yachts rocking in the afternoon swell.

Baggy always managed to come home with far more than he needed, simply because the variety on offer made it too good to miss out on anything. So he ended up becoming almost a vegetarian, especially in the hot, hot days of summer when a light meal was all he needed. Everything looked so wonderful he wanted to cook it all at once, so he invented his Market Day Pie, which lasted a lot longer than a day.

RECIPES

Market Day Pie ☐
(For 4 people)

Fresh Vegetables must be used in this recipe. For a vegetarian version simply omit the mince.

Utensils
1 large saucepan
1 frying pan
1 baking dish or casserole dish
2 gas rings
Oven gas mk. 4 - 5

Ingredients
5/6 new potatoes or 2 large old ones cut to size.
A few new carrots
A few sprigs of cauliflower or broccoli
2 large tomatoes, peeled and sliced
1 onion , quartered
1 courgette, sliced
Olive oil
1 clove garlic, crushed
8 oz (250 g) best mince (optional)
1 small tin red kidney beans
1 stock cube
1 tsp thyme
1 tsp oregano
Salt & pepper
½ tsp paprika
A few breadcrumbs

TIPS & TECHNIQUES

Vegetables have arteries *that run down them and carry their goodness, just as your arms and legs have arteries that carry your blood. If you want the goodness to remain in the vegetable then cut it in strips downward rather than across.*

A carrot sliced downwards before cooking will save more of its flavour than one cut across, which will 'bleed out' its goodness, especially when boiled. This is why we all hated those round knobs of school-dinner carrots yet in later life enjoy carefully cooked carrots.

If only using part of a vegetable such as a red or green pepper, or chili, cut a slice out of it from top to bottom rather than across the end (which is what comes naturally). You will find that the remainder will last very much longer before deteriorating.

Cabbage *can taste quite different depending on how you cut it.*

Fennel Seeds *are an indispensible addition to cabbage and cauliflower in any recipe. Once you start using them you will find cabbage decidedly bland without this addition, although you do not taste*

2 eggs beaten and mixed with 1 oz grated cheese

Method

1. Bring to the boil a large saucepan of salted water. Add the potatoes, and after a few minutes the carrots and cauliflower sprigs. Bring back to the boil and simmer for 10 minutes or until vegetables are just cooked. Remove them to the baking dish.

2. At the same time, dip the tomatoes in the boiling water; remove them with the point of a sharp knife, skin them, then chop them.

3. In a frying pan heat some olive oil and fry the onion and courgette until soft, together with the garlic.

4. Add the mince if using it and brown quickly. Add the tomato, kidney beans, crumbled stock cube and herbs. Simmer for 15 minutes. Taste and adjust the seasoning.

5. Add the mixture to the vegetables, piling the cauliflower and carrots in the centre and arranging the potato around the edge.

Sprinkle the breadcrumbs over the top and pour the egg-cheese mixture over it all.

the seeds themselves. Use just three or four seeds to start with.

Slice it very finely and steam it. Otherwise, throw it into fast boiling water for a few minutes.

For a change try cutting it in large chunks joined at the stem. Wash them well and boil it just like that. Pour off any liquid that collects and finish off with some butter, salt and pepper.

Steaming *is an excellent method of cooking vegetables since all the goodness is retained and they remain firm. (Be careful they are not too firm)!*

There are a number of steamers on the market, but for simplicity use a wire sieve that fits the top of a saucepan which will still take a lid on top.

Potatoes or a firm vegetable can be cooked in the water beneath whilst cabbage, spinach or broccoli – anything that would normally cook quicker than the vegetable underneath – can go on top and steam.

That way they should all be done in the same length of time. However, it does take a little practice to know what combinations of vegetables will cook well together.

7. Place in the oven for 30 – 40 minutes or until brown on top.

One should be able to taste the different vegetables rather than it being an amalgam, which is why it is preferable to separate them in the dish.

Braised Chard with Pistachio Nuts ✓∗

Chard stalks have a lovely nutty flavour, which is enhanced by the addition of a few shelled pistachio nuts.

Utensils
1 medium saucepan
1 gas ring

Ingredients
1 lb (450 g) chard
A small handful of shelled pistachio nuts
2 oz (56 g) butter or a mixture of butter and olive oil
Salt & freshly ground black pepper

Method

1. Wash the chard in plenty of fresh, salted water and tear off most of the green leaf, leaving just a little on each white stem. Chop the stems into 1" pieces, reserving the rest of the leaf for another dish.

Market Day Pie can be varied depending on the vegetables available.

Chard stalks or celery is a useful addition. They should be fried with the onion and courgette.

Jerusalem artichokes can be included but only a few or they will overpower the other vegetables. Add them to the water with the broccoli. In fact these two strong-flavoured vegetables complement each other.

They are completely different from the beautiful Globe Artichoke, yet their taste is very similar. It is an old-fashioned vegetable much used in the past, probably because it will grow in any back garden and goes on forever.

Now, people can't be bothered to peel and scrape these lumpy roots, but the distinctive taste is worth the effort now and then. Choose ones that are large and as smooth as possible and just chop off the bumps. They are delicious simply boiled and served with a parsley sauce.

Chunks of cabbage can be added with the potatoes but try to keep them together in large pieces joined at the stem.

Spinach can be prepared and cooked separately, drained, and then

2. Melt the butter and/or olive oil in a saucepan and braise the chard stalks in it with the lid on, shaking the pan and stirring now and then to stop them sticking.

3. When the chard is cooked (about 5 minutes), add the pistachio nuts, the pepper and a little salt if necessary.

Buttered Carrots Braised with Onion
✓ *

Utensils
1 small saucepan with lid
1 gas ring

Ingredients
A knob of butter and/or cooking oil
3 medium carrots, peeled and cut in strips lengthways.
½ onion, roughly chopped
Salt and pepper
A pinch of sugar or ½ tsp clear honey
Chopped parsley (optional)
Finely chopped hazel nuts (optional)

Method

1. Heat the butter and/or oil in the saucepan and add the carrots, onion and salt.

2. Put the lid on and cook over a low heat until the carrots are soft (about 10

added in a ring inside the potatoes.

Washing green leaves *such as lettuce, spinach or cabbage in salted water has a twofold benefit. The salt acts as a mild antiseptic, killing off any greenfly or larger bugs that might be lurking there. It also helps to crisp up the leaves, especially if they are allowed to soak for ten minutes or so.*

Cauliflower florets should always be washed like this.

Spinach stalks *make a useful addition to a number of dishes. When the green leaves have been torn from the stems they are usually simply discarded. This is a great waste, especially if they are fairly solid. Simply chop them up and add them to another vegetable dish, as in Market Day pie.*

Chard *looks like thick spinach with a wide flat white stem. It is a two-in-one vegetable, for the green part can be used exactly like spinach, and the stems make a delicious dish in their own right.*

Pistachio Nuts *are small, expensive, and very tasty. Their cost is perhaps why they are rarely used in cooking. The braised chard recipe opposite could be done with finely chopped brazil nuts, pine nuts or peanuts.*

minutes) shaking the pan now and then and checking that the carrots are not burning. The onion will give the carrots enough moisture to cook.

3. Towards the end of the cooking throw in the hazel nuts then add the sugar and finally the parsley just before serving.

Spinach in Yoghurt ✓ ☐
(Traditional Turkish recipe)

Utensils
1 large saucepan

Ingredients
1 lb (500 g) fresh spinach
2 heaped tbsp plain yoghurt
A pinch of grated lemon zest (see T & T)
½ clove crushed garlic
Salt & freshly ground black pepper

Method

1. Wash the spinach thoroughly in plenty of cold salted water and remove any thick stalks. Pile it into a large saucepan so that it cooks in only the water adhering to the leaves. Turn it over now and then with a wooden spoon. It is cooked as soon as it is reduced and softened.

Hazel Nuts, finely chopped, are a pleasant addition to the Carrot and Onion recipe.

Any vegetable is better for being braised or cooked in its own juices with a little oil. This way all the goodness remains in the dish.

It is the onion that gives the moisture to the carrots in the braised carrot recipe, and if you find it is still not moist enough add a little water and adjust the lid as needed.

Radish tops are another leaf that we normally throw away, but can be usefully combined with spinach or chard leaves. They can be a bit tough so use them sparingly.

Beetroot tops can be used in exactly the same way as spinach.

Yoghurt is generally thought of as a desert with various flavours added, but plain yogurt is a frequent accompaniment to savoury dishes in the Middle East and India.

It has cooling properties in itself when eaten, and can even be used externally to ease sunburn. The drink called Ayran in Turkey and Lhassi in India made from yoghurt mixed with water and salt is a traditional cure for heatstroke (and is good for hangovers too)!

2. Strain off the water, pressing it out with the spoon. Cut the spinach roughly on a board and leave it to cool.

3. Meanwhile, mix the yoghurt with the other ingredients in a bowl large enough to add the spinach when it has cooled.

This mixture improves with keeping for an hour or so when the ingredients have had time to blend.

It is an ideal way of serving a green vegetable on a hot day when you are tired of salads.

Tomatoes Stuffed with Bulgur ✓□

Utensils
1 saucepan
Small bowl
Small pie or oven dish to hold the tomatoes upright

Ingredients
3 large tomatoes
Olive oil
½ onion, diced
1 clove garlic, crushed
A handful of bulgur wheat
A few currents or sultanas
A few pine nuts, or other chopped nuts
1 pt (½ l) boiling water
Salt & pepper
Mint

There are a great many savoury dishes with yogurt and garlic and other ingredients, but anyone can make the simplest 'saramsaklı yoghurt' of Turkey or its equivalent: plain yoghurt flavoured with garlic. It is a simple accompaniment to any spicy grilled meat and in India is a cooling accompaniment to curry.

***Tsatsiki**, a traditional Greek recipe is basically the same as the Spinach in Yogurt recipe but with grated cucumber instead of spinach.*

The small Mediterranean cucumbers can be used without any preparation, but if using the large watery kind we know in England the grated flesh needs to be salted and the water squeezed out, then rinsed before using. It seems such a shame to get rid of all that lovely fresh cucumber juice but if you do not, then your Tsatsiki will be too watery. An alternative is to cut the cucumber in small chunks and put it in the yoghurt mixture without salting it – but eat it straight away.

***Lemon zest** is the peel of the lemon without any pith. It is usually finely grated from the fruit, but you may find it easier to cut a sliver from the end of the fruit with a sharp knife and chop it again finely. It is quicker than getting out the grater and having to wash it afterwards.*

Method

1. Cut a cap off the top of the tomatoes and scoop out the middle into a bowl, leaving a firm edge all around and on the bottom.

2. In the saucepan fry the onion in the oil until beginning to turn brown, adding the garlic towards the end of the cooking.

3. Meanwhile, chop up any large pieces of tomato in the bowl.

4. Add the bulgur to the frying pan and pour on the boiling water. Let it rest until all the water is absorbed. Add all the other ingredients except the mint.

5. When the mixture is quite dry and fluffy again, having absorbed the tomato juices, add the mint and pile it into the tomato cases. Put a little oil in the pie dish, place the tomatoes in it and dribble a little oil on top. Replace the tomato caps. Bake until the skins look soft but not collapsed.

Balsamic Vinegar has a mild subtle flavour quite unlike the harsh vinegar we were brought up with.

Large 'Beef' Tomatoes are best for stuffing, as they stay firm. If they have a bit of stalk on top, so much the better, as it gives the cap an attractive look.

Check the tomatoes for a good fit in the dish you are going to cook them in, so that they hold each other upright, before you put the filling in.

A grapefruit knife (slightly curved and serrated) is ideal for cutting around the tomatoes, and a teaspoon will scoop out the flesh. The hard central core can be discarded.

Traditionally the stuffed tomato recipe is done with rice, but bulgur is very useful because it does not need cooking; it just needs to absorb the boiling water.

Mint perks up the flavour of tomatoes, whereas the herb Basil softens the flavour.

CHAPTER 14:   BEAUTIFUL SOUP

After the long hot summer the rain came. It rained and rained and then the sun came out again as hot as ever, making the earth smell and bringing thoughts to Baggy's mind of green English fields and hedgerows.

"Good mushrooming weather," he said to himself, sniffing the air. He had been told of a place where mushrooms abounded – given the correct weather conditions and it was not far from where he was moored in a sheltered Turkish harbour.

Having made sure the anchor was secure, Baggy left *The Sea Crow* to fend for herself and took a bus-ride into the hinterland. Near an old village he spotted a field of short grass with a horse grazing peacefully in one corner. Where do you find mushrooms? 'In a field with a horse, of course,' he mumbled under his breath.

He hopped off the bus at the next stop and pushed his way through thorn hedges and over old dry riverbeds to the field in question and sure enough: there they were! First of all he found huge heads of old field mushrooms rotting away in the grass. But as he walked further, in no time at all he spotted the lovely pure white heads of the newborn field mushroom pushing its way through the turf with unbelievable strength. He picked and sniffed at the pink gills.

"Aah!" he sighed. "Unmistakably the real thing." Country born and bred, he knew a real mushroom from a toady look-alike!

He spent a happy morning rambling around, filling his plastic bags then made his way down to the village to await the return of the mid-day bus. The villagers were extremely interested in what he had in his bags and told him vehemently that he must not on any account eat these fungi – it would turn him mad. "Mad!" they repeated, rolling their eyes and making as if to fall on the ground with their hands to their heads in case he needed a demonstration to understand their language. They tried to take the bags from him, indicating he should throw the nasty things away. But Baggy clung firm to the handles, trying to assure them in his faltering Turkish that these were not mind-bending toadstools, but good eating mushrooms such as he had been brought up on and for which he had been longing for many a month now. The bus arrived and reluctantly the villagers let him go, but not without a final admonishment.

A little while later, having cooked all his mushrooms in a variety of ways and even having made some wonderful soup out of them, he returned to the field and collected another bagful. As before, he then made his way to the village for the return bus. The villagers greeted him with enthusiasm, patting his shoulder and staring into his eyes.

"How are you? Are you well?" they enquired solicitously.

"I'm well, very well," he replied cheerfully. Again they peered in his bag but a little more carefully this time, picking out some of the mushrooms and examining them in detail.

The next time Baggy went to what he now considered to be 'his' field he found it bare. Someone – or several people – had been there before him! The weather was right, the time was right: but the field was bare. "Oh well, it was good while it lasted," he said to himself resignedly as he made his way once more to the village. Although they were friendly enough, he sensed a slight embarrassment amongst his previous acquaintances and no one asked to look in his almost empty plastic bag. 'If only I had been clever,' he thought, 'and returned the second time with dark glasses, an obvious hangover and a stumbling gait!'

There would be no more mushroom soup, or mushroom anything. But now he realised he could make soup out of a great variety of vegetables, for he had worked out a basic recipe that he could adjust accordingly. When the weather was cooler a thermos of homemade soup was ideal for his travelling, and so much better than the packet variety.

RECIPES

Cream of Mushroom Soup ☐ *

Utensils
1 large saucepan with lid
Hand-blender or liquidiser
1 gas ring

Ingredients
8 oz (225 g) fresh mushrooms, chopped
½ onion, finely chopped
2 oz (56 g) butter
1 tbsp soya flour or plain flour
Salt & pepper
1 pt (450 ml) milk
1 pt (450 ml) water
1 chicken stock cube
A dash of dry sherry
A slurp of cream

Method

1. In a large pan melt the butter and briefly fry the onion. Add the chopped mushrooms, salt and pepper. Cover with a lid to 'sweat' them, but keep a close watch and stir frequently. Only a few minutes will be needed.

2. Sprinkle the flour over the mushrooms and stir it around to take up the fat, then add a little of the milk, stirring all the time to make a thick cream. Continue adding the milk and

TIPS & TECHNIQUES

All these soup recipes make approximately 2 pints (1 litre).

The Mushroom Soup recipe *opposite is out of this world if made with field mushrooms picked fresh in the early morning, but it is a lucky person these days who can find any field with mushrooms growing wild.*

Even scarcer are the people today who can with confidence recognise an edible field mushroom, and there are a number of toadstools that look similar but are poisonous.

In France, where the collection of all kinds of fungi for eating is a national pastime, every chemist has to be trained to recognise the varieties of fungi that may be brought in to them for verification, as well as being able to ascertain the symptoms of fungi poisoning. Even so, there are fatalities every year.

So unless you have confidence in your ability to know what's what use the shop variety and accept a reduction in taste value. Baggy once spent a sleepless night worrying that the mushrooms he had bought in the market and had eaten that evening might not be the true variety and it was not worth the worry.

stirring, then add the stock cube and water.

3. Bring it to the boil then simmer gently for 10 minutes making sure it does not boil over, as the milk will tend to make it do so. If it appears to curdle don't worry.

4. Use the hand blender in the saucepan to break up the mushroom pieces to the size you like, or liquidise the mixture and return it to the pan.

5. Add the sherry, adjust the seasoning and re-heat as required. Put a swirl of cream in each bowl before serving.

Mmm - wonderful!

Mixed Vegetable Soup □

Utensils
1 large saucepan
1 gas ring

Ingredients
1 potato, peeled and diced
1 carrot, peeled and diced
1 onion, chopped
Cabbage or cauliflower stalks, chopped
1 clove garlic, crushed
1 tsp mixed herbs
1 oz (28 g) butter or 2 tbsp oil
1 tbsp soya flour or plain flour

If you do use the big open flat variety of field mushroom, you may find the soup has a blue-black tinge although the taste is excellent! Use the pink gilled and mildly brown ones for preference.

All the Soup Recipes *have the same basic method, although they fall into two categories:*
a) Cream soups blended to a smooth creamy texture, and
b) Thick soups which still contain chunky pieces of vegetable.

Many people make soup by simply boiling the vegetables with the stock; but by 'sweating' them first in some butter or oil before adding the liquid makes it much tastier.

Sweating the vegetables means slightly cooking them with the lid firmly on the pan. Check now and then to make sure they are not catching on the bottom.

The flour is then used to absorb the fat so that it does not separate in the final product.

Ideally soup should be made with fresh meat stock but perfectly good soup can be made from stock cubes, which puts the whole idea of soup-making into a different category.

The range of stock cubes now

½ pt (275 ml) milk
1 chicken stock cube
1 pt (450 ml) water, preferably boiling
1 tbsp fresh parsley

Method

1. As before, prepare the vegetables then 'sweat' them all together in the pan with the butter or oil, including the mixed herbs and crushed garlic. This should only take 5 – 7 minutes and the vegetables should not be cooked through.

2. Sprinkle on the flour and mix it in to take up the surplus fat. Add the milk, stirring well to form a creamy texture.

3. Now add the water and stock cubes. Bring to the boil then turn down the heat and simmer for ½ hour.

4. Use the hand-blender or liquidiser to break up the vegetables into the size you want. Continue to cook for 15 minutes.

5. Add the fresh chopped parsley, adjust the seasoning and serve with a little extra parsley sprinkled on top, or with croutons to turn it into a meal in itself.

available means that you can vary the underlying flavour of the soup accordingly. Don't be afraid to mix and match them.

Vegetarians can use a vegetable stock cube and still have a tasty soup.

Proper stock *should be made from boiling bones, chicken carcasses and so on. It is so easy if instead of throwing the left-over pieces into the bin, you simply throw them into a saucepan. Roughly cut up a carrot and an onion, throw in some mixed herbs and a little salt and pepper; bring to the boil then simmer on a low heat for as long as you want.*

A slow-cooker is ideal for making stock in this way.

When ready, give it a good stir and pour the liquid into a bowl through a sieve. Now you can chuck the carcass in the bin because all the goodness is in your stock.

Large quantities can be made in less than an hour, frozen for future use in daily amounts or kept in the fridge and used as required.

Soya Flour *is better than plain wheat flour in soup-making as it adds flavour and nutrition. It does not thicken quite so much as wheat flour, but its main job is to absorb the*

Cream of Lettuce Soup ☐ *

Utensils
1 large saucepan
1 gas ring

Ingredients
1 small potato, peeled and chopped
½ onion, chopped finely
1lb (450 g) outside leaves of lettuce, chopped
Salt & pepper
2 oz (56 g) butter
2 tbsp soya flour or plain flour
1 pt (450 ml) milk
½ pt (225 ml) water (preferably boiling)
½ oriental chicken stock cube, or a piece of Star Anise
1 chicken stock cube
A little white wine (optional)
A dash of cream (optional)

Method

1. Sweat the onion and potato in the large saucepan with the salt and pepper, adding the lettuce leaves after a few minutes.

2. Continue as for previous recipes, sprinkling the flour, adding first the milk then the water and stock cubes. Bring to the boil then simmer very slowly for 20 minutes.

3. Blend as before, this time making

surplus fat, which it does very well.

An electric hand-blender is a wonderfully simple instrument that you can use straight in a saucepan or any bowl you happen to be using.

On a boat it will operate from a small inverter and sits neatly out of the way in its wall-attachment covered by its own measuring jug.

It will smooth out any sauce that might be a bit lumpy and is ideal for any recipe where a liquidizer would otherwise be needed. For soup-making it is ideal.

Everything is done directly in the saucepan. Afterwards, you simply run the end of it under the tap and pop it back in its fitting on the wall.

You can even get a special attachment that chops up parsley most efficiently.

A liquidiser requires transferring the soup in small batches from the saucepan to the liquidizer then into another receptacle and finally back into the saucepan. It entails complicated washing up so is hopeless in a small space.

The Vegetable Soup recipe can be varied depending on whatever vegetables you may have available. Add leftover peas or beans at the last

sure it is a smooth cream without any bits. Add wine and adjust seasoning; then continue to cook for 15 minutes.

Serve with a swirl of cream.

Leek & Potato Soup □

As above but substitute chopped and cleaned leeks for the lettuce.

Fresh Tomato Soup □ *

Utensils
1 large saucepan
1 gas ring

Ingredients
Butter and/or oil
1 onion, finely chopped
1 clove garlic
8 - 10 medium tomatoes, skinned and chopped
Salt, pepper and a little sugar
Stock made from stock cube and 1pt (450 ml) boiling water
A little mint or basil

Method

1. Fry the onion and garlic in the butter/oil until just turning brown.

moment. The thick stalk of the cauliflower is also excellent if you cut off the outside husk.

You can use any thick outside leaves of lettuce, cabbage or cauliflower so long as they are not too stringy.

It can be turned into Minestrone Soup by the addition of a tin of tomatoes, pasta and some Tabasco Sauce.

***Cutting vegetables:** page 116 of T & T describes how to cut vegetables lengthwise if you want to keep all the goodness inside, but for soup we need the flavours to exude, so cut crosswise your carrots, celery, or any other vegetable with arteries that run along their length.*

When sweating your vegetables for the soup recipe prepare the vegetables that take longest to cook first – potato, carrot – then any green stuff like cabbage or radish tops, last. That way they will all end up cooked to the same extent at the same time.

You can make soup out of anything, as the excellent recipe for lettuce soup shows. The flavour of the oriental stock cube is necessary in this recipe for lifting it out of the ordinary. If you can't find it, add a piece of Star Anise but remove it when you do the

2. Add the peeled and chopped tomatoes and the rest of the ingredients.

3. Bring to the boil and simmer very slowly for 15 minutes, then blend and adjust seasoning.

Jerusalem Artichoke & Mussel Soup *

Utensils
Saucepan
Bowl of cold water with lemon juice

Ingredients
2lbs (1 kilo) Jerusalem Artichokes
2 oz (56 g) butter
1 onion or white part of 1 leek, chopped
1 potato, diced
1 tbsp flour
1 pt (450 ml) milk
1 pt (450 ml) chicken stock
4 oz (250 g) prepared mussels (frozen or tinned)
A dash of dry sherry
Crème Fraise (optional)

Method

1. Peel and chop the artichokes and place them in the cold acidulated water to prevent them from turning brown.

2. Cook the onion or leek in the butter *blending.*

Dry Sherry *is a wonderful addition for giving any soup that up-market 'restaurant' flavour!*

Jerusalem artichokes *are a very good combination with mussels or any seafood.*

Fresh mussels *are a nuisance to clean and prepare so are best purchased ready prepared and frozen or tinned.*

Garlic Croutons *are a very useful addition to any soup and are very simply made.*

Cut stale white bread into little cubes. Gently fry plenty of garlic in a mixture of butter and olive oil being careful not to burn it. Remove the garlic.

Now fry your croutons in the garlic butter/oil. Remove them to some absorbent paper and sprinkle with a little salt.

For a delicate soup the garlic can be omitted.

Serve the croutons sprinkled into the soup, or in a separate bowl.

A hearty soup with croutons and a little cheese sprinkled on top is a meal in itself.

gently. Add the drained artichokes, celery and potato and continue to cook gently for 5 – 10 minutes.

3. Sprinkle on the flour, stir, and add the milk stirring all the time. Add the stock.

4. Bring to the boil and simmer slowly for 20 minutes.

5. Liquidise the soup; continue cooking for 15 minutes.

6. Add the mussels, and bring back to boiling point. Add the sherry and parsley. Remove from the heat and mix in the crème fraise.

Swirls of cream in a dark coloured soup like the Tomato Soup, and a sprinkle of parsley in a bland coloured soup such as the Artichoke and Mussel, make the dish so much more appealing to the eye.

CHAPTER 15: ENTERTAINMENT

Winter was coming on again. Although the weather was still fine and the winds more variable for sailing, there was a chill in the air that required long trousers and a jacket. Baggy decided to make his way to a sheltered town on the south coast. Several of his friends were heading that way too and he reckoned it would be as good a place as any in which to spend a sociable winter. It was an attractive town but did not afford much in the way of theatres, cinemas and such like, so 'the boat people' as the locals called them, got together and made their own entertainment.

Whether it was the quantity of cheap alcohol, the unaccustomed warmth in the winter sunshine, or the weekly barbecue that drew everyone together, who could say? The fact remained that more socialising went on than was good for anybody. The middle-aged hippie on *Rampant* was discovered ravishing the Norwegian lady from *Wilful* in the marina showers! *Lady 'A'* found many excuses to drop by in her dinghy to *Devil's Own*, and the attractive French lady on *Jig-a-Lig* had often walked home (the long way round through the sand dunes) with a randy *Sea Crow*.

Such tidal events were all part of a greater sphere of entertaining, mainly in the form of parties to which everyone brought along a bottle of wine and some food. It encouraged Baggy to extend his range of desserts, or puddings as he liked to call them. When he was on his own he never bothered with them much but with all this socialising going on he thought he had better look into the matter and get it sorted.

In fact he discovered that a number of the recipes he had already made could easily be turned into sweets – the pancakes, for instance, only needed a sweet filling instead of savoury; the sponge cake could be topped instead of filled, pastry could be made into a delicious tart rather than a savoury flan, choux pastry could be filled and doused in chocolate to make profiteroles.

He also came to appreciate how much more satisfying it was to cook for other people than for himself. He realised too that people eat with their eyes, so his food needed to look good as well as tasting good. Just a hint of colour in the form of a green herb or red paprika sprinkled on top of something savoury; a sprinkle of icing sugar or a grating of chocolate on a desert; a swirl of cream in the soup. People seemed to appreciate the food so much more when they knew a bit of home-made effort had gone into it, whereas anyone could go to a shop and buy something if they had the money. It was especially satisfying when his food produced such wonderful responses.

"It all tastes so good!" his guests would say. "How do you do it?"

He thought for a while, pondering on the fact that each person's cooking did in fact taste different even though they may have followed the same recipe. How could that be?

"Well, I don't know…" Baggy replied with his slow west-country drawl. "Maybe you just need to put a little love into it. Perhaps that is the secret ingredient."

RECIPES

Honeyed Fruit Salad ✓ *

<u>Utensils</u>
1 large bowl

<u>Ingredients</u>
1 banana
1 orange
1 pear
1 apple, preferably red-skinned
1 small tin pineapple chunks
A few red fruits (e.g. raspberries)
1 tbsp honey in a cup of warm water
A dash of orange liqueur

<u>Method</u>

1. Prepare the fruit, cut into bite-size pieces and place it all together in the bowl. Add some of the pineapple chunks, with a little of the juice and the orange liqueur.

2. Stir in the honey mixture, which should by now be more or less cold.

Crème Delight ✓ *
(4 servings)

<u>Utensils</u>
4 wineglasses

TIPS & TECHNIQUES

Fruit Salad is often all that is needed to finish off a rich meal, but a fruit salad can be plain as ditchwater or a delight of mixed fruity tastes. The inclusion of the honey sweetens it up and the liqueur makes it special.

Oranges for a fruit salad are best prepared in the following way, which makes the fruit appear more luscious and juicy:

Always use a sharp or serrated knife to make a clean cut. A blunt one will squash the fruit.

Peel the orange well, removing all the pith. This will be easier to do if you roll the orange around in your hands, squeezing slightly, before you begin.

After peeling, break it in half along a segment and cut out the core, removing any pips at the same time.

Place the orange flat side down on the cutting surface and cut straight across each way, ignoring the segmentation.

Apples with red skins add colour to the fruit salad, as does the addition of just a few red fruits.

Prepare them last as they will

Ingredients
4 oz (250 g) Crème Fraise
A few spoonfuls of homemade or good quality jam/preserve
Tubular wafers or sponge fingers

Method

1. Half-fill the glasses with the crème fraise.

2. Add a dessertspoon of jam/preserve and mix it carefully in swirls so that the different colours and tastes contrast each other. Take the spoon to the edge of the glass here and there so it looks good from the outside too. Don't overdo it!

2. Put a sponge finger or tubular wafer upright at the edge of the glass.

Mrs. B's Apple Crumble ✓ * ☐
(4 servings)

Utensils
A mixing bowl
A deep pie dish
Oven gas mk. 5

Ingredients
2 - 3 large apples
1 oz (28 g) granulated sugar

For the crumble topping:

discolour if left on their own.

Peel the apples if the skins are tough.

Remove the stones from plums or cherries for a fruit salad or the unwary guest may break a tooth!

Crème Delight *is as simple as a desert can be, yet it looks and tastes delicious. Serve it with a wafer or plain biscuit as it is rather rich. A sprig of mint or lemon balm on the top makes it seem special.*

Wipe the rim of the glasses with damp kitchen paper if they look messy.

'*People eat with their eyes*' *is a very true saying. Nowhere does it seem to be more important than in the case of desserts, which always tempt us before we have even decided on our main course.*

It all comes from that basic instinct of the hunter-gatherer, which no doubt protected our forbears from eating food that would not be good for them.

Colour is exceptionally important in food. The addition of a sprig of fresh green herb or a little red colour in a basically bland-looking dish will tempt us into wanting to eat it.

4 oz (110g) self-raising flour
2 oz (56 g) butter or margarine
2 oz (56 g) Demerara sugar
1 tbsp chopped hazelnuts or almonds (optional)

Method

1. Peel and core the apples. Cut them into slices and pile them in the pie dish with a very little water and the sugar.

2. Make the crumble by mixing together the flour and fat as though you were going to make pastry. Add the sugar and nuts (if using them).

3. Pile the mixture on top of the apple without pressing it down in any way.

4. Bake in the pre-heated oven, gas mk. 5 for ½ hour or until the top is crunchy and the apple cooked. The apple will just start to bubble up through the topping when it is ready.

Strawberry Sponge Flan *
(4-6 servings)

Utensils
Electric mixer or balloon whisk
Large mixing bowl
Sieve
1 sandwich tin lined with greaseproof paper

It also shows you care enough to want to make it appealing.

Crumble *makes a useful pudding especially if you do not have the time or energy to make pastry.*

It can go on top of any fruit, not just apple, though this is the traditional country recipe.

Apples *have a nasty habit of turning brown while you are preparing them. Putting them in a bowl of water to which you have added some lemon juice or an ascorbic acid tablet helps to prevent this.*

Otherwise just do it quickly, peeling them all first so that only the outsides are exposed to the air.

Sultanas *or chopped dates can be added to the apple to turn it into 'Dutch Apple Crumble'.*

Demerara Sugar *is the course light brown sugar often used in coffee. If you don't have any, white sugar will do.*

The addition of chopped nuts to the crumble gives it a nice crunchy texture as well as adding to the flavour.

Strawberry Sponge Flan*: The base of this flan is the same as the*

Oven gas mk. 4
1 small saucepan

Ingredients
For the sponge base:
2 eggs
2 oz (56 g) sugar
2 oz (56 g) self-raising flour

For the topping:
8 oz (225 g) fresh strawberries, or other fruit
Nappage, OR:
1 tsp cornflour
1 tbsp sugar
1 tbsp red-currant jelly
1 cup boiling water

Method

1. Whisk the eggs and sugar until they are light and fluffy.

2. Fold in the flour gently but quickly, shaking it through a sieve as you go.

3. Pour it into the lined flan dish and bake it in the oven for 20 minutes until firm to the touch and well risen.

4. Remove it from the tin and place it with the papered side uppermost on a wire rack to cool. Remove the paper.

5. If you do not have Nappage mix the cornflour and sugar in a cup with a

4 x 4 Sponge Cake on page 86, but using half the ingredients and only one sandwich tin.

Nappage is a product available in France, where many country housewives make tarts with the fruit available from garden or country market. It replaces the cornflour mixture in the recipe opposite and, if available, is certainly superior.

Any fruit can be used for the flan. Peaches or apricots cut in half-moons look lovely, with the red tinge from the centre blending with the redcurrant mixture.

Decorate the sponge flan with a small flower or a sprig of lemon balm. (It does not have to be edible)! A swirl of whipped cream will do well, but remember to have some extra for serving.

Lemon Balm is a lovely herb to have in the garden, and once planted will never leave you. Its other name is Melissa; honeybees love it. The leaves have a distinctly lemon-taste and are useful for decorating desserts.

Golden Syrup is a peculiarly English ingredient which is almost unobtainable anywhere else – so visitors are often asked to put a can in their hand-luggage (well-sealed of

little cold water then fill the cup and pour it into a small saucepan. Bring it to the boil stirring all the time and making sure there are no lumps and that the final mixture is clear in colour.

6. Pull the stalks off the strawberries and cut them in half lengthways. Place the sponge on a serving plate, and arrange the strawberries in a pattern on the top.

7. Pour the Nappage or cornflour mixture, carefully over the top, making sure that all the fruit is covered and you have a nice level surface on top. Remove any that runs over the edge.

West Country Treacle Tart ☐ *

Utensils
Mixing bowl
Flan dish
1 saucepan
1 gas ring
Oven gas mk. 4

Ingredients
Pastry made from 3 oz (85 g) plain flour, 3 oz (85 g) SR flour, 3 oz (85 g) butter or margarine, 1 tbsp sugar, a little grated lemon rind (optional).

course).

Even in England it is not like it used to be. Now produced as a thin pourable liquid, it is easier to use but is similarly thin in taste. You used to have to fight with it to get it out of the tin!

The Dutch make a passable kind of syrup but otherwise the nearest equivalent found abroad is probably Maple Syrup.

Pastry-making Tips *can be found on pages 51-55 – but don't forget the main one: –*

Keep cool and do it fast!

Pieces of pastry left over *from lining the flan-dish for the treacle tart can be rolled out and cut into strips, then twisted and placed in a lattice effect across the top.*

Stick them down with milk, cold water, or a bit of the filling. They will look even better if you brush them with a little milk to make them shiny. A mixture of egg and milk is even better.

When cooking for guests *always think about what they will like.*

Equally for guests *there are one or two etiquette tips that seem to*

For the filling:

3-4 tbsp Golden Syrup
1 level tbsp soft brown sugar
3 oz (85 g) walnuts, broken up (a small handful)
1 tbsp soft white breadcrumbs
2 eggs, beaten

Method

1. Roll out the pastry on a floured board and line the greased flan-dish with it.

2. Warm the syrup in a saucepan with the walnut pieces and sugar. Remove it from the heat, and stir in the breadcrumbs and the beaten eggs.

4. Fill the pastry case with the mixture, and bake for ½ hour in the oven, gas mk. 4 until it is golden brown and just firm on top.

have been forgotten in the 21st century.

As a guest, never start your food until everyone is served and the cook is seated. Even if the cook encourages you to start, do so hesitantly – they are probably only being polite.

Remember to pass around the serving dishes and don't forget the cook who may otherwise end up with little to eat while the guests are eating and chattering away happily with the serving dishes at the other end of the table.

If one person is eating much more slowly than the others, pace yourself, lay down your knife and fork for a minute until they catch up.

If you are a fast eater, putting your knife and fork down with a happy flourish while everyone else is only halfway through will only make the others uncomfortable. Again, pace yourself to the other guests.

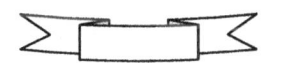

INDEX TO TIPS & TECHNIQUES

This index is only for items mentioned in the Tips & Techniques.
See also Table of Contents for specific recipes.

Aioli	90, 113
Alcohol	73, 79
Allspice	85
Aniseed (liquor)	63-64
Apples	59, 134-5
Aubergine	104
Bacon	8, 56
Basil	95-96, 122
Bay	34
Beans, dried	24-25
Beetroot tops	120
Brandy	85
Breadcrumbs	37
Bulgur	11
Butter	17, 105, 126, 130
Cabbage	57, 116-7, 118, 129
Cake	82-84, 85, 86, 87
Capers	96-97
Chard	118
Chicken	27, 36-7, 45
- stock from carcass	127
- giblets	36
- liver	36
Chili	76, 109, 116
Chutney	98
Cinnamon	59, 75, 85, 86
Coconut milk	69
Coriander leaf	20, 67-68

Coriander seed	92-93
Crème Fraise	111
Croutons	130
Cucumber	121
Cumin	34, 75
Curry Powder	69
Dolmades	57
Duxelles sauce	47, 113
Eggs	15-16, 18, 90, 91
- to separate the whites	18-19
- pickled	91
Fennel seeds	116-7
Fennel bulb	67
Fish	62-68, 69-70, 79, 112
- to gut	62
- sardines	62, 63
- bones	62-63, 64
- anchovies	64
- to debone cooked	65
- to choose fresh	65-66
- farmed	66-67
- pâté	109
Fish slice	14
Flour	83
- self raising	83-84
- soya	127
Fruit salad	134
Frying pan	14, 16, 17
Garlic	10
- clove	10
- crusher	10
- prepared	42-43
Ginger Beer	97
Ginger	43
Golden Syrup	86, 137-8
Gougière	111-2
Gravy	26, 31, 42, 48, 52
Hand-blender	128

Harissa	43, 76
Hazel nuts	120
Herbs	24, 55, 73, 74-75, 79, 106
- fine	19-20
- mixed	9, 24, 106, 127
Jelly	94-95
Jerusalem Artichoke	118, 130
Lamb	48
Leeks	10
Lemon	67, 94, 111
- juice	90, 94, 95, 136
- zest	121
Lemon Balm	135, 137
Liquidiser	128
Liver	106
Margarine	53, 105
Marinade	74
Marmalade	92-94
Mayonnaise	90, 109, 113
Meat (general)	23-4, 31, 33-34, 36, 47, 73-74
- minced	52, 74
Mint	20, 122
Mixed dried fruit	84-85
Mushrooms	9, 42, 125, 126
Mustard	55, 78-79
Nappage	137
Oil	9, 35, 90
- olive	16, 17, 36, 130
Onion	9, 120, 127
- to chop	9
- rings	9
Oranges	92, 106, 134
Ovens	27, 38, 58, 105
- yacht	32-3
- microwave	32, 105
Pancakes	46-47
Paprika	75

Parsley	19-20, 51, 104, 110, 111, 131
Pasta	8, 9, 24, 101, 102, 103, 104, 106
Pasties	51-52
Pastry	27, 48, 51-2, 84, 136, 138
- tips to make shortcrust	52-5
- filo	47-48
- borek	47-48, 58
- puff	112-3
- choux	112
Pâté (general)	79
Pepper (ground)	67
Pistachios nuts	121
Pork crackling	34-35
Potato	9, 18, 56, 68-9,
- roast	31-2
- creamed	68-69
Prawns	109-110
Pressure cooker	26, 93
Quail	27
Rabbit	77-78
Radish tops	120
Raisins	85
Rice	8, 9, 38, 43, 44, 45, 106,
Ring mould	112
Rosemary	24, 34
Scones	86
Scones	86
Seafood	68
Sherry	24, 43, 130
Slow Cooker	26, 69-70, 77-78, 127
Soup	58, 125-131
Spatula	84
Spices (general)	73-5, 79
- pickling	91
Spinach	118-9
- stalks	119
Sponge cake	86-87, 136-7
Star Anise	69

Steaming	117
Steam-roasting	38
Stock cubes	9, 33, 42, 126-7
Stock	127
Stuffing (general)	36, 37, 38, 122
Sugar	59, 92, 93
- castor	84
- Demerara	136
Sultanas	59, 85, 86, 136
Tabasco	109
Tarragon	42
Thyme	24, 106
Timing	101
Tinned food	25, 130
Tomato	122
- to remove skins	17
Tsatsiki	121
Vegetables	39, 118
- to prepare	116, 129
- to steam	117
- in soup	126, 129
Vinegar	90, 91, 122
- Balsamic	122
Whisks	18
White Sauce	104-5
Yoghurt	73, 120-1

Please review this book.
Reviews are very useful for spreading the word.

If you would like to contact me directly with questions or comments then please Email me at:

sarita@saritaarmstrong.co.uk

Or visit my website at:

www.saritaarmstrong.com

info@sifipublishing.co.uk

SIFIPUBLISHING
WWW.SIFIPUBLISHING.CO.UK

www.sifipublishing.co.uk

ABOUT SARITA ARMSTRONG

Sarita Armstrong spent over 20 years living on sailing boats in the Mediterranean, firstly on her own 26ft catamaran which she sailed mostly single-handed from Spain to Turkey; then on 60ft sailing yachts, often catering for charterers. She sailed as crew on a 54ft sailing yacht across the Atlantic from South Africa to Brazil and now lives on a barge in France. Prior to sailing, she owned her own restaurant for twelve years in Devon.

Notes

Notes

Notes

Notes

Notes

Lightning Source UK Ltd.
Milton Keynes UK
UKOW07f1930131217
314422UK00005B/615/P